THE LOVE BOMB

and other musical pieces

By the Same Author

POEMS
The Memory of War
Children in Exile
Out of Danger

LITERATURE
An Introduction to English Poetry

ESSAYS ON ART
Leonardo's Nephew

LECTURES
The Strength of Poetry

TRAVEL
All the Wrong Places

GARDENING
A Garden from a Hundred Packets of Seed

THE LOVE BOMB

and other musical pieces

James Fenton

VIKING
an imprint of
PENGUIN BOOKS

VIKING

Published by the Penguin Group
Penguin Books Ltd, 80 Strand, London WC2R ORL, England
Penguin Putnam Inc., 375 Hudson Street, New York, New York 10014, USA
Penguin Books Australia Ltd, 250 Camberwell Road, Camberwell, Victoria 3124, Australia
Penguin Books Canada Ltd, 10 Alcorn Avenue, Toronto, Ontario, Canada M4V 3B2
Penguin Books India (P) Ltd, 11 Community Centre,
Panchsheel Park, New Delhi – 110 017, India
Penguin Books (NZ) Ltd, Cnr Rosedale and Airborne Roads,
Albany, Auckland, New Zealand
Penguin Books (South Africa) (Pty) Ltd, 24 Sturdee Avenue, Rosebank 2196, South Africa

Penguin Books Ltd, Registered Offices: 80 Strand, London WC2R ORL, England

www.penguin.com

First published 2003
1

Set in 10.75/14.75pt Trump Mediaeval
Typeset by Rowland Phototypesetting Ltd, Bury St Edmunds, Suffolk
Printed in Great Britain by Clays Ltd, St Ives plc

A CIP catalogue record for this book is available from the British Library

ISBN 0-670-91288-3

To Craig Raine

Contents

Preface   ix

THE LOVE BOMB   1

HAROUN AND THE
SEA OF STORIES   65

THE FALL OF JERUSALEM   171

Acknowledgements   183

Preface

It never seems to happen that a poet sits down and writes a libretto without first being commissioned. Perhaps we should make this happen. Perhaps we, the poets, should begin by asking ourselves: what sort of opera, what sort of musical drama, should we like to see? Then we should go ahead and perform our half of the task, leaving it up to whatever composer came along to set our work to music, or not, as may be.

. . . Or not – it is that negative possibility, hanging in the air, that gives us pause. Suppose I did all this, and then nothing happened? We look at our colleagues, the composers, and they too seem in need of reassurance. Suppose they took a year, two years, ten years to compose an opera, and then nothing happened to all their work, not to mention all our work for them? How should they, how should we feel about that? Better then not to set pen to paper without a decent commission.

This is the common state of affairs, but there is no pressing artistic reason for it to be so. Indeed when we look at the history of opera we find that there have been times when the work of the librettist has enjoyed an existence quite independent of the individual composer. This happened inadvertently in the cases of Büchner and

Maeterlinck, who wrote in the nineteenth century the texts for two of the greatest operas of the twentieth: *Wozzeck* and *Pelléas et Mélisande*. But it also happened by design in the case of Metastasio, who, in the eighteenth century, wrote libretti which were immediately considered works of art in themselves, and which many more than one composer set to music.

Today, while it is not surprising to find that an individual poem has been set to music by more than one composer, we tend to think of a libretto as a unique drama to be set in a unique fashion. Obviously Shakespeare's dramas might attract more than one composer, but the fact that there is more than one *Turandot* and more than one *Barber of Seville* may strike us as curious and somehow against nature. The fact that Metastasio's *L'Olympiade* was set by, among others, Vivaldi, Pergolesi, J. C. Bach, Arne, Cimarosa and Paisiello seems utterly outlandish. Could adequate singing texts have been in such short supply?

The answer may be that they were not. What was different was the attitude of the time. Today there is nothing to stop a composer writing another *Wozzeck* – nothing except the attitude that says: this thing, done once, should never be repeated. In the same way, there is nothing to prevent the librettist from initiating his own opera – nothing except the custom and the attitudes of our time, our patterns of commission and patronage.

2

All the works here, the two libretti and the text for an oratorio, were the result of three quite different commissions, and yet when I look at the upshot I see that all three pieces share an overt theme, in a way that was never planned. That theme is fanaticism.

In the oratorio, the Jews who refuse to bow to a Roman yoke are seen from the point of view of their historian, Josephus, who made his own compromises in his life, and was keen to justify them. I chose the subject because the commission was for a small oratorio to mark the millennium. Most millennium commissions were designed to celebrate twenty centuries of achievement. But I took the view that the millennium might be considered as a scaring date, an ominous marker, and I suggested as much to Dominic Muldowney.

We were writing for choirs in Leeds and Southampton, for the kind of great chorus that was formed to sing Handel and the grand oratorios of the nineteenth and twentieth centuries. I thought of *Judas Maccabaeus*, of *Elijah*, of *The Dream of Gerontius* and *Belshazzar's Feast*. Josephus and the story he had to tell seemed easily to measure up to the grandeur of such conceptions, however our oratorio turned out in the execution.

Haroun and the Sea of Stories, the children's novel, is the book with which Salman Rushdie, after the *fatwa* against him by the Ayatollah Khomeini, asserted his right to continue as a free spirit. The story is dedicated to Salman's son Zafar, whose name is incorporated as an acrostic in the dedicatory verse, a verse which I have taken care to preserve in my libretto – it provides the opening and concluding thoughts of the opera.

Zembla, Zenda, Xanadu,
All our dream-worlds may come true.
Fairy lands are fearsome too.
As I wander far from view
Read and bring me home to you.

Salman the writer was taking the opportunity, in the face of the personal catastrophe that had befallen him, to explain to his son why the mullahs might be against him, and why it was worth standing up to them. At issue was the freedom of the imagination.

When the composer Charles Wuorinen proposed the story as the subject of an opera for adults, and I was approached to versify it, it seemed natural to treat the commission as if it were for a musical. I consulted with the composer, and turned in a text which was to all intents and purposes a musical with numbers – even though I knew that the music that would eventually be set to these words would be quite different from anything one encounters on the commercial stage. The point was to find a useful dramatic idiom. This piece was commissioned with help from a number of foundations, for performance at the New York City Opera.

The Love Bomb differs from the other two commissions in that it is an original story and not an adaptation of anyone else's text. Unless, that is, you take it as a version of one of the oldest and most frequently set opera stories, the story of Orpheus and Eurydice. A composer came to me with an idea for an opera about a

modern cult. A woman goes into a cult and a man tries
to get her out, and somebody towards the end of the story
gets killed: that was the outline, as put to me. At some
stage I mentioned to the composer that it sounded like a
version of the tale of Orpheus, in which Eurydice doesn't
want to leave the underworld (as, although I hadn't
thought of this, she doesn't want to leave in the Offen-
bach version).

I devised a scenario, after which the composer men-
tioned that he would like the story to have a strong overt
homoerotic theme – it was time, he felt, that opera grew
up and treated such matters. Happy to comply, I dropped
two characters, gave new prominence to a third, and
abandoned the Orpheus analogy – only later to realize
that (in certain versions of the myth) Orpheus does
indeed turn, after losing Eurydice, to homosexual love.
That is why he is killed by the Maenads, who object to
his songs on the subject. (But there are quite enough
Orpheus operas already.)

In the meantime I had been thinking about, and reading
about, the world of the Christian cults. Among the terms
that cropped up in the books I found were 'flirty fishing'
and 'love-bombing'. Flirty fishing is a technique for
attracting converts to the cult by holding out an offer
of sexual favours. Love-bombing is designed to force
adherence to the group: the convert is love-bombed by
being showered with more love, affection and attention
than he could have believed possible, by the various
members of the cult; then suddenly all this affection is
withdrawn completely; the convert is devastated, and
will do anything to work his way back into the favour of
the group.

These two pieces of jargon suggested the whole situation. A woman comes fishing for her ex-boyfriend, on the instructions of the cult to which she belongs. The boyfriend follows her, for he has been asked by her parents to get her out of the cult, and he genuinely hopes to re-establish, if not their love affair, at least their friendship. The young man is love-bombed – loved to pieces, then excommunicated – and, in the dreadful aftermath of his exposure as a spy with a homosexual past, is forced to prove himself, to regain the trust and affection of the group. He is sent out, in turn, on a fishing expedition, to bring *his* former boyfriend into the orbit of the cult. The two men arrive at the cult headquarters just at the moment of a planned Armageddon.

The writing of this story, the devising of a convincing theology for the leader of the group, the elaboration of the characters involved, the writing once again of 'numbers' for each key situation – engaged and engrossed me, and I looked forward, on handing in the script, to making the revisions which I expected the composer to require. Unfortunately it was at this stage that we reached what he called 'an unforeseen impasse' – namely that the composer felt that this text, though it was exactly what he had envisaged, and his music would 'work to each other's disadvantage' and 'show each other in the most unfavourable light'.

So it happened that I was left in the position I mentioned at the beginning of the preface: I had written the libretto to a commission which evaporated, and I finished and revised it ultimately as a demonstration of what I believed an opera or musical drama could be.

3

The commission had evaporated. The composer had evaporated. The first thing I did to my libretto, when the air cleared, was type in the titles and numbers of the musical 'numbers', so as to establish more clearly what they were. This may seem a small matter. It felt exhilarating, since I was now alone with my project and there was no collaborator to consider or consult. I had written numbers, and numbers I intended to have.

The next task was to find a composer, but to find a composer for what? For a musical drama of some kind, clearly, but perhaps after all not an opera. It happens there is no English word for the object we are left with, once we expunge the term opera from the script. *Una dramma per musica* (a drama for or through music) is the phrase I would like to render into English, but it does not translate itself with any ease. It is not something poised half-way between opera and musical, as if the one were serious and the other light; it is not a *semiseria*, a half-serious entertainment. As for the word 'musical', one would be happy to use it, as long as the word was not going to mislead, to create wrong expectations as to idiom. But the musical *does* have its own history and its own parameters.

As it happens, the problem of defining the dramatic genre I was interested in has its parallels in the world of music. Contemporary, classical, experimental, rock, crossover, jazz, fusion, world – there is often something about these terms that fails to rise to the occasion. On the other hand, there is also often a way of pointing to the kind of thing one means. In musical drama, is the piece intended for miked or unmiked voices? That is a good indicative question, since unmiked voices really must have an operatic training. Are we thinking of singers who can act or of actors who can sing? What is the composition of the band? What is the hoped-for venue?

A series of such questions can give a good notion of the kind of music to be expected. For instance, if the text is written for actors who can sing, then the music will not ask the performer to do with her voice the kind of horrible things that, say, Tippett asks for in *The Knot Garden*: 'Ca-A-a-ATCH-a-NI-i-I-I-gg-er-bYee-the-TOE!!' No actor *can* do it, and no actor wants to do it, and quite right too. On the other hand, there are plenty of singers who can do desirable things that no singing actor can begin to emulate.

The kind of Christian cult I based my story on takes much of its style from television – from pop videos and music shows. And it was always envisaged that the music of the opera would, in some way, at some remove, represent the music of such cults. That is why the text gives the composer at least the opportunity (whether or not it is taken up) to include songs in popular forms, along with hymns and chants and various forms of dramatic speech. There seems to be no reason why what was written in the first instance for the opera house should not transfer, should not perhaps do better, in another kind of theatre altogether.

It would be nice to be able to say in conclusion that such questions have been settled, but I hardly like to jinx what seems a very promising beginning on a new tack. For the world of musical drama seems as full of setbacks as that of film. *Haroun* itself has, at the time of writing, been scheduled twice, and twice postponed, by the New York City Opera, the soloists engaged and disengaged, director and designer hired and then cut loose. *The Love Bomb* has its new composer, John Harle, but awaits a commission. But at least the librettist has this luxury that, his work now done, he can present his text to the reader, and beg – not for indulgence, but for a little imagination in the reading. Nobody would believe that the dog ate my homework. But that the dog ate my opera house – *twice* – might well be believed.

THE LOVE BOMB

A musical drama by John Harle

If any man come to me, and hate not his father, and
mother, and wife and children, and brethren, and sisters,
yea, and his own life also, he cannot be my disciple.

Luke 14, 26

Dramatis Personae

Martin
Anna
John
Brother Paul, a cult leader
Brother Simon, an elder of the cult
Police officer
Male and female cult members
Police and firemen

ACT ONE

Scene One

At a pub table.
Martin and John.

JOHN:
  I'm not objective.
  I've told you that before.
  I've got my own perspective
  And it's the opposite of yours
  And I mistrust myself
  And I mistrust my motives overall
  But Anna has left you, Martin,
  She's left you for Brother Paul.

MARTIN:
  You think she's having an affair.

JOHN:
  No more than all the rest of them.
  It's like a harem over there.
  They worship him
  And they'll do anything at all
  To efface themselves
  To abase themselves
  To embrace their Brother Paul.

MARTIN:
  I feel I ought to follow her
  As if she'd gone out for a walk
  And simply failed to reappear.

Even as we talk
I feel a panic coming on.
I feel that I've no business to be here.
I should be looking for her.
I should be raising the alarm.
I should be out there with a torch
In case she's come to any harm.

JOHN:
What makes you think
She'd thank you for your pains?
She's run away.
She's run away and slammed the church door in your
    face.

MARTIN:
You've always hated her.

JOHN:
No, but I was jealous once.
I'm not objective, as you know.

    [They part.]

1. *Love and be Silent*

JOHN: [SOLUS]:
'Love and be silent':
That was a good idea,
A harsh resolve,
A chilly way to start the year.

Frosty philosophy,
Cold comfort for the heart.

Suffer to some purpose.
Let the bleeding start.

Scene Two

In a sitting-room.
Martin and Anna.

MARTIN:
I know if it's over it's over.
I don't want to speak about us.
But you know how your father and mother –
You know how they fuss.
You know they get worried. They wonder
If it's something they've said or they've done.
They feel you're becoming a stranger.
(And) they don't know what's wrong.

ANNA:
Who doesn't know?

MARTIN:
Your mother. Your father.

ANNA:
Who is my father?
Who is my mother?

MARTIN:
Anna!

ANNA:
What do you mean:
'If it's all over'?

MARTIN:
I said I didn't want
To bring that up again.
It isn't why I'm here.

ANNA:
Why are you here?
Why are you here, Martin?
Who sent you here?

MARTIN:
Nobody sent me here.
Anna!

2. *Speak to Me*

Speak to me, Anna, like you used to do.
Speak to me once again.
Speak to me just this once, even though we're through.
Try to explain.

It may not help. It may not tide me over
This drift, this deadness where you used to be.
But there's a way of letting down a lover.
Let me down more tenderly.

And there's a way of letting down a lover
Without this dreadful slamming of the door.
And I have friends who, after it was over,
Have become friends once more –

Live in the same place, hang around together,
And know each other's partners, and they don't fight.

And some – you wouldn't know they'd once been
   lovers.
It's water under the bridge. And that's all right.

It's water under the bridge. It's only normal.
It's a case of that was then and this is now.
But when I stare down from the bridge at all that water
It doesn't seem to make the blindest bit of sense,
   somehow.

ANNA:
   I've been busy.

MARTIN:
   You don't have to lie to me!

ANNA:
   No, it's more than busy.
   It's like being loved for the first time
   And being able to love in return.
   It's like having a family
   Where there was none before.

MARTIN:
   Anna!

ANNA:
   You asked me to tell you
   And I'm telling you.
   It's like
   Who is my father?
   Who is my mother?
   And suddenly the answer comes in a flash.

MARTIN:
My father is Brother Paul.
My mother is Brother Paul.
My aunt and uncle
My sister and my brother –
Everyone is Brother Paul.

ANNA:
You don't have to yell.
You asked me and I'm telling you.
Listen to me, Martin.

3. Love and Death

You know what London is like.
Sometimes you wonder why you bother –
Getting up, getting ready,
Going through the rigmarole
As if you were dressing a paper doll:
This is Anna's underwear.
These are her shoes.
This is her office outfit –
Skirt and blouse and matching bag
Held in place by paper tabs.

Anna is going to work.
This is Anna at the bus-stop.
Here comes Anna's bus.
Oh look.
Anna didn't get on the bus.
What's happened?
Maybe Anna is going crazy.
Maybe Anna's lost her mind.

Don't go down that street, Anna.
Don't go down that street.
That's where all the murderers live.
Well, maybe it's a murderer I want to meet.

Don't go down the towpath, Anna.
Don't go along the canal.
That's where all the accidents happen.
Treat me to an accident. Be my pal.

> 'Cos one door opens on love
> And one door opens on death.
> And one door opens on the lift shaft.
> Turn the handle. Hold your breath.

Don't go out at night, Anna.
Don't go out in the dark.
That's when all the skeletons
> Rattle their bones
> Rattle their bones
> And drag you down to Davy Jones.
Well, maybe Davy Jones would be quite a lark.

> 'Cos one door opens on love
> And one door opens on death
> And one door opens on the lift shaft
>> On the lift shaft
>> On the lift shaft
Turn the handle, hold your breath
Death or love
Love or death
Every door means death or love.

MARTIN:
You scare me.
You scare me when you talk like that.

ANNA:
Maybe I scare myself.
Maybe we *should* be scared
When we look into our souls.

MARTIN:
Is that what they've been teaching you?

ANNA:
Is that what they've been teaching you?
Is that what they've been preaching at you?
No, it's something I've learned for myself.
Come with me.
Come with me to Brother Paul.

Scene Three

> *A church in a converted cinema.*
> *Dancers and Singers.*

4. Chorus: He is the Beat

CHORUS:
Beat, meditation, dance and light.
Beat, meditation, dance and light.
He is the light.
He is the beat,
The runway on the funway to the one-way street.
[I said]

Beat, meditation, dance and light.
Beat, meditation, dance and light.
He is the way.
He is the truth,
The saviour on the wavelength with the emphasis on
    youth.
The emphasis on youth.
The emphasis on truth.
The saviour on the wavelength with the emphasis on
    youth.
[I said]
Beat, meditation, dance and light.
Beat, meditation, dance and light.
Dance to the beat.
It comes from the street.
Liberation, Salvation is a one-way street.
There's no turning back.
There's no turning slack.
There's no turning back 'cos it's a one-way street,
A runway,
A funway,
A one-way street.

5. *Magic Hands*

GUITARIST (Brother Simon):
    You walk the stony places.
    You walk fair and tall.
    Along the lonely ridges
    You hear the ravens call.
    But always there is Someone
    To catch you when you fall.

Magic hands
Will catch you when you fall.
Oo oo.
Magic hands
Will catch you when you fall.

You ride the lonely canyon.
You go for many a day
Forlorn but not forsaken.
Your sorrow makes you stray.
But always there is Someone
To wipe your tears away.

Magic hands
Will wipe those tears away.
Aa aa.
Magic hands
Will wipe those tears away.

And some are born to falter
And some are born to fail
And some are born to stumble
Along the darkening trail

Along the darkening trail, O Lord,
Along the darkening trail,
There's many you will find, My Lord,
Along the darkening trail.

You walk the stony places.
You go through many lands.
You cross the frozen river.
You cross the parching sands.

And no one sees that Someone.
No one sees those magic hands.

Magic hands
No one sees those magic hands
Oh Lord.
Magic hands
No one sees those magic hands.

6. Chorus: Christ is My Idea of Glamour

CHORUS:
Christ is my idea of glamour.
Christ is where I want to be.
Though I squint and though I stammer
Christ will make a star of me.

By his birth and by his passion,
By his suffering in the end,
Only Christ can set the fashion.
Only Christ can set the trend.
Amen.

ANNOUNCER (Brother Simon):
Ladies and gentlemen, I give you, the man you've all
been waiting for – the one and only Brother Paul.

[Dry ice. Lights. Brother Paul is dressed in
white suit, black shirt and dark glasses.]

7. Coming Together

BROTHER PAUL:
   Coming together in love
   Coming together in hope
   Coming together in ecstasy
   That's what coming together should be.

   Love is a draught of fire
   Hope will fan the flame
   Fan the flame of ecstasy
   That's what coming together should be.

   Coming together in sin
   Burning our sins away
   Burning our sins in ecstasy
   That's what coming together should be.

   I am a man of sin
   You are the children of God
   We are the children of ecstasy
   That's what coming together should be.

   Coming together with fire
   Fire and wind and flame
   Burning our shame in ecstasy
   Coming together with you, with me.

   Coming together with God
   Coming together with me
   Coming together with ecstasy
   You in God and God in me.

I am a man of God
I am a man of flame
I am a man of ecstasy
I am a man with God in me!

8. *Chorus: Turn*

CHORUS:
Turn from the cradle, turn from the hearth,
Turn from your house and home,
Turn to the love, turn to the wrath,
Turn to the terror to come.

Turn from your father, turn from his hand,
Turn from his cuffs and blows,
Turn to the God who will smite the land
With a thousand, thousand more than those.

Will you pause at the threshold, hesitate
When you hear your mother cry?
Turn to the plague, turn to the scourge,
Turn to the blood that is in the sky.

Turn from the streaming, streaming blood,
Turn to the terror to come,
Turn to the plague, the famine and the flood,
The flood which will wash away your home.

This is the flood. This is the wrath.
This is the hovering dove.
These are the flames of ecstasy.
This is the terror of love.

9. *The Insect Sermon*

BROTHER PAUL:

And we are the insects in the sight of God.
And we are insects.
Every saint was an insect.
Every apostle too.

When I was a child
I collected insects
And pinned them to a balsa-wood board
And I killed them with a chloroform swab.

Christ was an insect
Just like us
And they took him
And pinned him to a board

And Christ flapped his wings
Just as my insects used to do
And the vinegar in the sponge
Was the chloroform swab

And he pressed his nose into the sponge
And he breathed in the vinegar
He breathed in the vinegar
Of the father who hated him

But had sent him this vinegar
This vinegar of mercy.
And he said Why?
Why have you forsaken me?

Does every father hate his son?
Does every son look up one day
As Isaac looked up
And saw his father Abraham with his knife –

The knife raised high,
The son pinned down
On the balsa-wood board,
The insect ready to die?

How could our father Abraham
Find strength to pierce his son like an insect
Unless a kind of hatred
Slumbered in his heart?

And God said: Search out
And find that hatred for your son,
That insect of yours –
Search out that hatred for your insect son.

And Abraham said to the Lord:
Where, Lord, where shall I find it?
And the Lord said:
There, where your love is, there you will find your
    hatred.

And Isaac looked up
And he saw that his father Abraham had found the
    hatred,
Had found the hatred slumbering in his love
And Isaac knew he was an insect, no more than a
    vinegar flea.

As Christ breathed in the chloroform,
As Christ breathed in the vinegar mingled with gall,

He knew he was an insect in the sight of God
As we are insects in the sight of God.

This is the mystery of love.
This is the mystery slumbering in God's love.

10. Chorus: Farewell

CHORUS:
Farewell to the love of the world.
Farewell to the love of our home.
Farewell to the love of our family.
Farewell to the love of our friends.

I am turning my face to the fire.
I am turning my face to the flood.
I am turning my face to the love and wrath,
To the love and wrath of God.

Oh burn me in your fire.
Oh drown me in your flood.
Consume me in the love and wrath,
In the love, in the wrath of God.

Scene Four

At a pub table again.
Martin and John.

JOHN:
Well, then, she's lost it.
She's gone mad for Brother Paul.

MARTIN:
  Don't say that.

JOHN:
  She has signed away her sanity
  And she wants you to do the same.

MARTIN:
  She wanted me to go along
  And see for myself.
  And her parents wanted me to.

JOHN:
  Her parents?
  I thought you and Anna were through.
  What's all this about her parents?
  What are they to you?

MARTIN:
  They simply asked me.
  They wanted me to rescue her.

JOHN:
  Rescue her? Rescue?
  Rescue her from what she wants to do?
  Rescue her from deserting you?
  Rescue her from hurting you?
  What is this foolishness?
  Can you not see?
  They want you to save their family.
  And she –
  Maybe she doesn't know
  What there is in store

But maybe she wants to hurt you
Just a little more.

11. *Let's Go Over It All Again*

Some people are like that.
They split up and then they think:
Hey, maybe we haven't hurt each other to the
    uttermost.
Let's meet up and have a drink.

Let's go over it all again.
Let's rake over the dirt.
Let me pick that scab of yours.
Does it hurt?

Let's go over what went wrong –
How and why and when.
Let's go over what went wrong
Again and again.

We hurt each other badly once.
We said a lot of nasty stuff.
But lately I've been thinking how
I didn't hurt you enough.

Maybe there's more where that came from,
Something more malign.
Let me damage you again
For auld lang syne.
Yes, let me see you bleed again
For auld lang syne.

MARTIN:
John, I can't let Anna drop.
I almost feel I've pushed her into this.

JOHN [*handing Martin a file of clippings*]:
I've brought you the cuttings you asked for.
Here they are.
You'll see what Brother Paul is like.
Once you join you never leave.
Once you join it's goodbye dad,
Goodbye mum.
Goodbye pounds.
Goodbye pence.
Goodbye soul.
Goodbye sense.

They say that salvation is a one-way street
And they mean what they say.
They have their methods. That's why you seldom meet
Anyone who got away.

[*They get up to leave the pub.*]

12. I'm Not Objective

Listen to me.
If you have to go with Anna
There's nothing I can do.
Maybe you have to try at least.
I could be wrong.
And I admit that I have selfish reasons too –
Reasons to regret her hold over you.

I'm not objective.
I've seen you suffering too long.
It drives me nuts.
I feel the blade
Twist in my guts.

I'm not objective.
I've watched her take you up
And put you through the mangle
And that outrages me.
And that's – well – that's a sort of angle.

It made me feel for you
Far in excess of what I should.
It made your suffering real for me –
Perhaps too real for my own good.
I can't conceal from you
I'm not objective, I've a point of view.

Don't sign your soul away, Martin.
Don't sign your soul away.

End of Act One

ACT TWO

Scene One

The church as before.
Brother Paul, Martin, Anna, cult members.

13. You are the Rock

BROTHER PAUL:

When Jesus came to gather his disciples
Down by the snoring Lake of Galilee
D'you think his folk were happy to lose their Simon,
To say farewell to the sons of Zebedee?

Zebedee wept and tore his hair and garments
And smeared his face with ashes from the hearth
And Simon's mother screamed among the potsherds
When Simon followed Jesus down the path.

Zebedee wept to see his sons desert him
For he was frail and getting on in years.
Soon he'd be left with nobody to help him
And so he cursed his offspring through his tears.

And Simon followed Jesus to the lakeside
And still his mother screamed and called him home.
And Jesus said to Simon: Thou art Peter
And Peter shalt thou die for me in Rome.

You are the Rock. They are the Sons of Thunder,
No longer now the Sons of Zebedee
And you shall leave your mothers and your brothers
Beside the snoring lake of Galilee.

CHORUS:

We are the Rock. We are the Sons of Thunder.
And we have turned our backs on hearth and home.
We are the saints and we shall soon be martyrs
In Ephesus, Jerusalem and Rome.

BROTHER PAUL:

Now Mary called her other sons together
And she had grown so thin and pale and sad.
She told her boys to take control of Jesus
For Jesus had undoubtedly gone mad.

And so his brothers sent a line to Jesus
To tell him they would wait for him outside
But Jesus knew that they had come to get him
And this is how the Son of Man replied.

He said:

Who is my mother? Who is my brother?
Who is my sister? I am alone.
These are my followers and my believers
And this is all the family I own.

This is the Rock. He is my mother.
These are the Sons of Thunder. They're my kin.
These are my sisters. These are my brothers.
And this is where my mission will begin.

CHORUS:
   We are the Rock. We are the Sons of Thunder.
   And we have turned our backs on hearth and home.
   We are the saints and we shall soon be martyrs
   In Ephesus, Jerusalem and Rome.

BROTHER PAUL:
   Martin, you have been with us all this time.
   Now you must tell us how you find us.
   Now you must share your feelings with us.

14. The Love Bomb

MARTIN:
   It's just as Anna promised me.
   It's exactly as she said.
   So many friends and so much love.
   It's like a love bomb in my head.

   It's like a love bomb in the brain.
   It's like a love bomb in the heart,
   Blowing all my past away,
   Blowing my old life apart.

   The happiness I once enjoyed
   Seems such a small, a trivial thing.
   The friendships and the family
   Seem so remote and posturing.

   It's like a putting into port.
   It's like a stepping off a train,
   Like an embrace and like a dream,
   Like finding something lost again.

Like finding that a wall is false
And watching as the panel slides
And stepping into a hidden space
And finding what the panel hides:

The hidden life, the hidden love,
The looming trees, the brilliant lawn
Reflected in the looking-glass,
The garden at the break of dawn.

BROTHER PAUL:
Well, it is true that we have given you
All the love we can
And yet I sometimes wonder . . .

MARTIN:
What do you wonder?

BROTHER PAUL:
I wonder what you are holding back.
I wonder why you find it
So hard to give,
So easy to receive.

MARTIN:
But I have given you all my love.

BROTHER PAUL:
All your love?
Was that *all* your love, Martin?
I thought I saw
Through a chink in the door
Another room, another love,
A love that you were holding in reserve
In case this love turned sour on you.

I thought I saw another love,
A love perhaps from long ago,
A different love, perhaps a secret love,
Hoarded and treasured in the soul,
In case this love walked out on you,
In case it turned its back on you,
As certain loves are liable to do.

Oh – 'I have given you all my love' –
All my love trips easily off the tongue.
Judas Iscariot gave Jesus all his love
But still he held some back
Just in case.

MARTIN:
Brother Paul!

BROTHER PAUL:
I see the comparison offends you.
But it is true.
Judas Iscariot loved Jesus once
Enough to leave his family and home.
But still he kept a little in reserve,
A little pot of coins he buried in a cave.

MARTIN:
If it's a matter of money –

BROTHER PAUL:
It's not the money.
It's the meaning of the money.
It's not the little pot of coins.
It's the meaning of the little pot of coins.

MARTIN:
  You think I would betray you,
  Brother Paul?

BROTHER PAUL:
  Someone will betray me, Martin,
  That much is certain.
  Someone who loves me will betray me.
  Why should it not be you?
  When first you loved Anna,
  Did you not betray a friend?

MARTIN:
  Anna!

ANNA:
  It is true.
  John loved you, and you betrayed him.
  You loved John, and you betrayed him.
  And sometimes as we lay in bed together
  Sometimes when we were making love
  I thought: how easy you found it, this betrayal.
  If you betrayed John, why should you not betray me?

MARTIN:
  I never betrayed you.

ANNA:
  Maybe you're betraying me now.
  Maybe you're betraying all of us.

  Why did you follow me, Martin?
  Why did you follow me here?
  Was it the love of Jesus?
  Or was it something less sincere?

Who was it who put you up to it?
Who set you on my tail?

MARTIN:

Wait, it was *you* invited me.

ANNA:

I don't remember it like that.
I remember you hated Brother Paul.
Why would I invite you?
Somebody sent you.
That's what I've always felt about you.
Somebody sent you to keep an eye on me
To spy on me.

Who sent you here, Martin?
Who sent you here?

MARTIN:

Nobody sent me here.
Your father and mother were worried about you,
But nobody –

ANNA:

My father and mother:
You're working for my father and mother.
You are spying on me,
Spying on us,
Spying on Brother Paul.

MARTIN:

It's not spying.
I came here out of concern.

BROTHER PAUL:
So everything you said just now
Was a lie.

MARTIN:
What do you mean?

BROTHER PAUL:
About the love you had found
And the love you had given –
It was all a lie.

MARTIN:
No. I was surprised.
I –
Look, if you don't want me here,
I shall go.

BROTHER PAUL:
Go? Just like that?
You are not going anywhere
Until we find out who you are working for.

MARTIN:
You can't do that to me.
I am free to go any time I want.

[*The male acolytes move to block the doors.*]

It's a free country.
I can go any time I want.

BROTHER PAUL:
Who are you working for, Martin?
Who are you working for?

ANNA:
  Judas Iscariot!
  Judas Iscariot!

CHORUS:
  Judas, Judas, Judas.

MARTIN:
  It's a free country.
  I can walk out the door.
  You can't stop me.

  [In a panic, he makes to go.]

BROTHER PAUL:
  Deal with him now.
  Deal with him.

  *[The men overpower Martin, and knock him
  out with a chloroform swab.]*

Scene Two

  *At the country house headquarters of the cult.
  Martin is being held in a basement cell.
  We can hear the cult members, off-stage,
  practising a hymn.
  A male orderly brings in a tray of food, while
  another keeps watch at the door.*

MARTIN:
  Where am I?
  How long have I been here?
  Will nobody speak to me?

*[The orderly leaves the room, without
acknowledging Martin's presence.]*

But I *know* where I am.
I know where I must be.
Sometimes a car goes by
And I can hear the gravel on the drive.

The sound of someone raking leaves,
Scraping the ground . . . the mopping of a floor,
The hasty steps along a corridor –
The noises of a grand estate.

At dawn, somewhere nearby
An airport opens its runways to the sky.

I should be honoured after all
To be the guest of Brother Paul,
To be invited to his country place.
But it doesn't feel like an honour.
It feels like a sore head after a bad fall,
A catastrophic fall from grace.

15. The Vapour Trail

Now through the grating of my cell
I look up at a strip of autumn sky
And often, chalked across the blue,
There's a vapour trail,
A vapour trail . . .
And then, I don't know why,
John, my dear friend,
I start to think of you.

Dawn brings these planes from distant lands,
Red-eyed tycoons from far-flung ports of call.
Dawn lifts the luggage through the flaps
On to the carousel
The carousel
And wakes the baggage hall.
Dawn will bring you, perhaps.

Perhaps that vapour trail is where
Your plane passed over me here in my jail.
That line is the trajectory
Of your breakfast tray,
Your breakfast tray.
Perhaps that is your trail
And you look down on me.

Look down on me, my friend, look down
And think of me now as I think of you
And think of us as we were then
From your vapour trail,
Your vapour trail . . .
Your line of chalk on blue.
Think well of me again,
      My friend –
      Whatever hurt I may have done,
      For I intended none.
      Forgive the hurt that I did not intend
      And let it mend.
Think well of me again.

      [Enter Brother Simon.]

Who are you?

BROTHER SIMON:
I am Brother Simon, your advocate.

MARTIN:
A lawyer?

BROTHER SIMON:
Not exactly.
It is my job to plead for you
With Brother Paul
And I have to tell you
The case looks bad.

MARTIN:
How so?

BROTHER SIMON:
Anna and the brethren searched your flat.
They found these cuttings in a file
And they found these letters
From a man called John.
Who is this John?

MARTIN:
A friend.

BROTHER SIMON:
More than a friend, I think.

MARTIN:
What business is it of yours?

BROTHER SIMON:
 I told you.
 I am your advocate,
 The only friend who can help you out of this.
 We have to know
 Why you were spying on us.
 You were working for John.
 The cuttings file proves that.
 But who is John?
 And why is he working against us?
 You have to tell us this.
 You have to tell us everything.

MARTIN:
 And if I refuse?

BROTHER SIMON:
 To refuse is to say:
 I am still working against you,
 Working against God's will,
 Working against Brother Paul.
 Is that the message you wish to send?

MARTIN:
 No.

BROTHER SIMON:
 John was your lover, was he not?

 *[Brother Simon places a tape-recorder on the
 table, and turns it on.]*

MARTIN:
 John was my lover.

BROTHER SIMON:
   And would be still,
   If he could have his way.

MARTIN:
   And would be still, perhaps,
   If Anna had not had her way.

BROTHER SIMON:
   That sounds bitter.

MARTIN:
   I've no right to be bitter.
   It was I who walked out on John.
   Why did you say 'And would be still'?

BROTHER SIMON:
   There was a recent letter in your flat.

MARTIN:
   May I read it?

   [Brother Simon hands him the letter.]

Scene Three

   John, solus.

16. *You've Disappeared from the Screen*

JOHN:
   Where are you, Martin? Where have you been?
   Like some night-flying long-haul jet from JFK,
   You've disappeared from the screen.

I'm almost ashamed
The number of messages I've left
On your machine.
You've disappeared from the screen.

You've disappeared from the screen.
One moment you were there and we were talking.
Next thing I knew
You'd vanished in the blue.
Now when I try to phone I feel I'm stalking.
Arrest me, do.
Arrest me for pestering you.
We used to be inseparable.
Have I done something irreparable?
Am I suddenly unclean?
You've disappeared from the screen.

You've disappeared from the screen.
The Archway bus was asking after you.
And Clissold Crescent
Looked thoroughly unpleasant
The last time I came wandering idly through
And gave a glance
At your unwatered plants –
The trailing petunias
Looked frail and impecunious.
I could not intervene.
You've disappeared from the screen.

> I'm not a monk.
> I've been out once or twice,
> Got a bit drunk
> And met somebody nice

But I knew all the time
I'd never find
What I was thinking of –
Something a little less like sex
And more like making love
Something profound for a change –
Something better than those nefarious gymnastics
With coked-up blokes in various elastics –
That was never my scene.
You've disappeared from the screen.

You've disappeared from the screen.
And London seems so meaninglessly leafy
And all the men
Irrelevant again –
The tall, the small, the epicene, the beefy.
I'm stuck without you.
I'm out of luck without you.
Consider it from *my* angle
In your Bermuda Triangle.
Is it nice or is it mean
That you've disappeared from the screen.

Scene Four

*In the main hall of the cult's country
headquarters.*
*The elaborate interior suggests a
nineteenth-century stately pile, which has been
fitted out to form a kind of throne-room. The
cult members, men and women placed apart,*

stand in formation around the throne, which
will be occupied by Brother Paul.
Brother Paul, Brother Simon, Martin, Anna,
cult members.

17. Chorus: Oh Sing the Song of Moses

CHORUS:
Oh sing the song of Moses,
The song of the Son of Man.
He comes to reap his harvest,
His sickle is in his hand.

He reaches for the cluster
And finds the time is good.
High as a horse's bridle
There flows the river of blood.

It floweth from the winepress,
The winepress of his ire.
It floweth from the winepress
To the sea of glass and fire.

And we are clothed in linen
And our harps are in our hands
And we shall see the Seven Plagues
Visited on the land.

And we shall hear the trumpets
And we shall hear the drums.
We shall be girdled all in gold
When Armageddon comes.

BROTHER SIMON:
  I bring to the Tent of Testimony
  A penitent sinner.

BROTHER PAUL:
  Is he truly a penitent?

BROTHER SIMON:
  I have examined him
  And do believe so.

BROTHER PAUL:
  Martin, you have been examined
  And found a penitent.
  Kneel before me and bow the head.

18. Worship Me

God says:

Not until you worship me,
Worship me,
Worship me,
Not until you worship me
Shall the soul of sin be free.

Worship is empty of design.
Worship is empty of desire.
Worship is an emptying.
Worship is a cleansing fire.

Worship me. I am the wind.
Worship me. I am the rain.
Worship me. I am the fire –
The fire upon the darkening plain.

Worship me. I am the word.
Worship me. I am the breath.
Worship me. I am the life.
Worship me. I am the death.

I am the death in Golgotha.
I am the death upon the tree.
I am the tomb. I am the shroud.
I am the body. Worship me.

End of Act Two

ACT THREE

Scene One

In John's Archway flat, London.
John is making coffee for Martin.

MARTIN:
Good old Archway.
I never thought I'd live to say
The words.
It sounds absurd.
But often when they kept me in that cell
I thought of you,
I thought of us –
I thought of hopping on the Archway bus
Back then, when we got on so well –

JOHN:
Milk?

MARTIN:
And Archway seemed the dullest of all dumps –

JOHN:
One lump or two?

MARTIN:
You don't buy sugar lumps!

JOHN:
You don't know what I do.
You forget –
You've been away.

You've been away for a year and a day
Without so much as a by-your-leave.
     [Seriously]
So now they trust you again.
They've let you out on parole.

MARTIN:

Now I'm a man on a mission.
I have to trap a human soul.

JOHN:

To trap a particular soul
Or will any soul do?

MARTIN:

To trap a very particular soul –
They've ordered me to come back with you.

     [John laughs.]

JOHN:

Dead or alive!
I'm flattered. But I decline.
What could they want with me?
They know that I detest the lot of them.
They know that I'm the enemy.

MARTIN:

They think that I've a power over you.

JOHN:

Now then, in that they may be right.

MARTIN:

And Brother Paul – he has a way with him
When he gets someone in his sights.

I'm scared of him.
The more I see his plan unfold
The warier I become of him.
There's something cold,
Something akin to murder in his eyes
But it's a murder that he offers you
As if it were a prize,
As if you were supposed to say:
Yes, murder my soul,
Murder my soul and make my day.

JOHN:
Get out now, while you can.

MARTIN:
I want to.
There's only one thing stopping me.

JOHN:
Anna.

MARTIN:
It's not quite Anna any more.
It's more the promise that I made.
It's like a pride in finishing a job.
I'd like to take her back home and then
I'd cheerfully never see Anna again.

JOHN:
Is this a labour of love
Or a labour of hate?

19. *If I Left Her There*

MARTIN:
   If I left her there,
   I'd feel that I had left her there to die.
   There's a pestilence in there.
   They're doomed.
   You only have to look them in the eye.
   It's like an endgame.
   It's like they're staring at the sky
   Searching for a sign
   Searching for the line:
   The End is Nigh.

JOHN:
   They're dangerous
   And what you are doing is dangerous,
   Dangerous for you,
   Which makes it dangerous for me.

   If I went back there with you
   I would contact the police first
   And tell them what I was going to do.
   I'd take no chances with Brother Paul.

Scene Two

> Back at the cult headquarters, where the
> windows in the great hall have been covered
> with wire grilles. A table has been set up beside
> the throne, on which a large punchbowl has
> been placed.

Martin, John, Brother Paul, Brother Simon,
Anna, cult members.

20. Chorus: Christ was Crucified in Sodom

CHORUS:

Christ was crucified in Sodom
And the corpses lined the streets
And the Sodomites made merry
Cracking nuts and swapping sweets.

And the corpses lay unburied
Three whole days and three whole nights
For the corpses were the prophets
Who had lashed the Sodomites.

They were men who came in sackcloth
And their mouths were full of fire
And they shut the skies of heaven
With their wisdom and their ire.

They were men who came in sackcloth
Through the fire and through the flood
And they spread a plague in Sodom
And the water turned to blood.

So no rain could fall on Sodom
While the prophets prophesied
Till a beast came up from Hades,
Fought the prophets, and they died.

Came the cloud and came the thunder
And the cisterns filled with rain

And the Sodomites were dancing
In the Cities of the Plain.

Came the thunder, came the lightning,
Came a voice from Heaven that cried:
Come up here, my slaughtered prophets,
To the wound that is in my side.

To the wound and to the wisdom
To the welt and to the weal,
Come up here, my slaughtered prophets,
And the Lamb shall break the seal.

Came the lightning, came the earthquake
And the prophets rose on high
And the Sodomites were slaughtered
In the ruins where they lie.

Christ was crucified in Egypt.
Pharaoh laughed to see him die.
Christ was crucified in Sodom
And they mocked his agony.

This is Egypt. This is Sodom.
Listen to the thunder peal.
We are saints and we are prophets
And the Lamb shall break the seal.

BROTHER PAUL:
Step forward, John.

Friends, this is John,
The friend of Martin,
Anna's friend.

I saw John in a dream
And I said: John, John,
Why do you persecute me?
Why do you long to destroy what you could love?
When you see a rose, do you tear it to pieces?
When you see a kingfisher, do you reach for a gun?
Pity the rose. Pity the kingfisher.

And John said to me:
Paul, Paul,
Does the rose ask mercy of the whirlwind?
Does the kingfisher cry to the eagle:
Pity me, I am a kingfisher?
Does the fire forgive the granary?
Does the flood spare the villages of the plain?

The scorpion says: I am a scorpion.
The tiger says: I am a tiger.
Only man is a riddle.

And I said to John in my dream:
Tiger and scorpion, eagle and whirlwind,
Fire and flood, what is your name?

And he told me the number of the letters of his
    name.
He told me the number of the letters of his name.

JOHN [*interrupting*]:
And you awoke. And it was all a dream.

And you awoke, Brother Paul, and it was all a dream.
The revelation was a dream.

And you awoke to a world
In which there was a man whose name you knew
Who despised you with all his heart.
And you thought:
I shall invite him to that temple of mine,
That prison-temple where I lock up my worshippers
And maybe he will worship me
Or maybe I shall deal with him.

I see that all the windows are barred
And all the doors bolted.
They are not barred against burglars.
They are barred to keep your worshippers in.
Worship me or else, the windows say.
What kind of temple is that?
What kind of worship is that?

I see a table set with a great bowl –
A sort of loving cup.
What sort of love is in the bowl, Brother Paul?
What sort of potion?
There is death in the bowl.
There is poison in the bowl.

And what is this I smell on the air?
There is petrol on the air.
There is murder and conflagration on the air.
You are a murderer, Brother Paul.
First you murder the soul,
Then you murder the body.
Then you plan a conflagration –
As if the fire will absolve you.

BROTHER PAUL:
Deal with him, Brother Simon.
Deal with the Antichrist.

[*At this exact moment, the great windows of
the hall are lit up by searchlights, and there are
blue flashing lights outside. Brother Simon
hesitates.*]

POLICE:
Open up. Open up.
Brother Paul, we have a warrant for your arrest
For false imprisonment.

BROTHER PAUL:
Brother Simon, set fire to the fuses.
Set fire to the fuses.
Let the Last Things begin!

[*Brother Simon goes up the great stairs, and
starts to set light to the upper floor. The police
begin knocking the door down, and breaking
the lower windows. As they do so, the Chorus
are singing in the background, while they begin
taking the poison.*]

21. Chorus (reprise): Farewell

CHORUS:
Farewell to the love of the world.
Farewell to the love of our home.
Farewell to the love of our family.
Farewell to the love of our friends.

I am turning my face to the fire.
I am turning my face to the flood.
I am turning my face to the love and wrath,
To the love and wrath of God.

Oh burn me in your fire.
Oh drown me in your flood.
Consume me in the love and wrath,
In the love, in the wrath of God.

MARTIN:
Anna,
Come with us now
Before it is too late.

ANNA:
Let go of me,
Antichrist, Antichrist.
You and your Satan-lover John,
You and my mother are poison to me,
You and my father are poison to me,
Poison to me,
Poison to me,
You and your lover are poison to me.

MARTIN:
Anna, don't –

  [*Anna is dousing herself with petrol.*]

ANNA:
I am turning my face to the fire!
I am turning my face to the fire!

  [*She is engulfed.*]

BROTHER PAUL:
Anna has chosen the Way.
Anna has chosen the Cup.
Anna has chosen the Call.

MARTIN:
Go poison yourself,
Go poison yourself, Brother Paul.

Poison yourself.
You poisoned my life long ago.
Poison yourself.
Make sure you do it well.
Drink long, drink deep and drink yourself to Hell.

BROTHER PAUL:
Antichrist, I drink to you!

> *[Brother Paul drinks the poison.*
> *The police break in and rush Martin and John*
> *out of the collapsing house.]*

Scene Three

> *In front of the burning remains of the house.*
> *Police and firemen at work in the background.*
> *John and Martin.*

JOHN:
Martin –

MARTIN:
Don't tell me I did everything I could!
Don't tell me that.

I don't want to hear.
I don't want sympathy.

JOHN:
I wasn't going to offer sympathy.
I was going to say
The officer said
They would let us go home soon.
Where will you go?

MARTIN:
Where will I go?
How do *I* know where I'll go?
Oh, leave me alone.
Leave me alone.

　　　[*Martin solus.*]

MARTIN:
It's true I don't know where I'll go
Or what I'll do.
How strange this is
And how horrible
As if she'd hung a piece of carrion around my neck
And said: wear that, wear it forever,
Wear this death of mine around your neck.

I can't face my flat.
Her fingerprints are all over it.
She turned the whole place upside down
Looking for evidence against me.

How thoroughly she hated me.
How thoroughly she hates me still
Alone in her circle of Hell.

Oh I can feel her hating me.

[*John and the Officer.*]

JOHN:
Officer,
I'm worried for my friend.
He shouldn't be left alone tonight.
Not after seeing Anna go like that.
I'm afraid he'll do something stupid.

OFFICER:
Could you put him up?

JOHN:
Of course.

OFFICER:
Why don't you speak to him?

JOHN:
I've tried.
Maybe he'll listen to you.
Tell him he mustn't be alone tonight.

OFFICER:
I'll see what I can do.

[*Officer and Martin.*]

OFFICER:
You've a place to go tonight?

MARTIN:
Yes.

OFFICER:
  Anyone there?

  [Martin is silent.]

You know you shouldn't be alone tonight.
You've had a shock. You've had a scare.
There's a delayed reaction
In cases such as this
And I should feel responsible
If anything should come amiss.

MARTIN:
  You think I might kill myself?

OFFICER:
  The strangest people do.
  But I should just feel happier
  With someone looking after you.

MARTIN:
  Well, if I did do something,
  I'd be entitled.

OFFICER *[sharply]*:
  Oh, you'd be entitled.
  You know what I wish
  More than anything in the world?
  I wish, when young lads like you
  String yourselves up,
  You'd spare a thought for the likes of us –
  The ones who have to cut you down.
  Do you think we don't wake screaming in the night?
  Do you think we forget your faces?

Do you think you're entitled to haunt us
For the rest of your lives?

> *[Martin hides his face.*
> *The officer continues mildly, after a pause.]*

Your friend seems kind.
He's got a level head.
I asked him if he'd mind
Offering you a bed.

MARTIN:
What did he say?

OFFICER:
He's got a spare bed.
He's happy to put you up.

MARTIN:
He said that?

OFFICER:
Talk to him yourself.
I'll fetch the driver.

> *[John and Martin.]*

22. Let it Mean Everything

MARTIN:
The officer said
You had a bed for me.
JOHN:
It's true.
Don't you remember?

MARTIN:
Yes, I remember our old bed.
But I'm afraid
If I come back with you
What it would mean.

JOHN:
Let it mean nothing.
Let it mean
The night was cold –
We shared a bed.
A cold night calls for company.

MARTIN:
I could have done that once,
Not now.
Not after all I've put you through.
If I go back with you
It would have to mean everything.

JOHN:
Well then,
Let it mean everything.
I'm on for that as well.
I'm on for 'everything',
Martin.
Can't you tell?

Let it mean everything.
Give everything a go.
I'll settle for everything.
I'd gamble everything on just one throw.

MARTIN:
It would have to mean everything.
It would mean that I was coming back again for good.
It would mean that we were starting again,
Starting from scratch –

JOHN:
What's wrong with that? Perhaps we could.

MARTIN:
It would have to mean everything.
It would have to mean everything.
    [With a sudden vehemence]
And I can't do it.
I mustn't go back.
Leave me alone, John!
For God's sake leave me alone!

    [The officers return and open the car doors.]

OFFICER:
Okay gentlemen,
We're taking you back to London.
Where do you want dropping off?

JOHN:
Archway for me.

OFFICER:
And what about Martin here?
Archway for you?

    [Martin is silent.]

Now remember what I said.
I should feel responsible.
You don't want me to feel responsible, do you?

MARTIN:
No, you are right.
I don't want you to –
I don't want anyone to feel responsible.

John, does your offer still stand?

> *[John is silent.*
> *Martin becomes agitated.]*

John?
Does your offer still stand?

JOHN *[with mild exasperation, after a pause]*:
What do you think?

MARTIN:
I think the night is cold
And a cold night calls for company.

JOHN *[laughing]*:
That was the password.
You've remembered the password!

OFFICER *[to the driver]*:
We'll be dropping these two gentleman at Archway.
Then you take me to Scotland Yard.

MARTIN *[to John]*:
I'm glad I remembered something.
To tell the truth,

A moment ago, when the officer asked me,
I couldn't remember my own address.

I don't know where or who or what I am.

Finis

HAROUN AND THE SEA OF STORIES

An opera by Charles Wuorinen

Based on the novel by Salman Rushdie

Dramatis Personae

Haroun Khalifa
Rashid, his father
Soraya, his mother
Mr Sengupta, a neighbour
Mrs Sengupta
Announcer
Two men with moustachios
Butt
Snooty Buttoo
Iff
Princess in Rescue Story
Mali, a Floating Gardener
Bagha and Goopy, Plentimaw Fish
The King of Gup
Prince Bolo
General Kitab
Khattam-Shud, the Prince of Darkness
Princess Batcheat
Chorus of citizens of Alifbay, Guppees, Chupwalas,
oarsmen, birds, heralds, cheerleaders, etc.

ACT ONE

Scene One
In the Sad City of Alifbay

SORAYA:
Zembla, Zenda, Xanadu:
All our dream-worlds may come true.
May come true.
They may come true.
All our dream-worlds may come true.

HAROUN:
That was my mother singing
In the sad city of Alifbay
And the smoke of the sadness poured away
Poured away
From all the sadness factories
Sadder than song
Sadder than song
Sadder than the seas where the glumfish swam
And something went wrong
One day
Something went wrong
And cut the thread of my mother's song.

SORAYA:
Zembla, Zenda, Xanadu
Zembla, Zenda . . .

HAROUN [*speaking*]:
   As if someone had thrown a switch!

   My father noticed none of this.
   He was too busy.
   Telling stories every day
   Hour after hour.

   Myth and magic, wicked uncles,
   Cowards, heroes, catchy tunes,
   Brand-new sagas, ancient legends,
   Gangsters in yellow check pantaloons.

RASHID:
   Oh, I am the Ocean of Notions.
   I am the Shah of Blah.
   The Source of the Sea of Stories
   Is roughly speaking where we are.
   I'm the guru of the Gulf of Gumption
   With a hundred-mile attention span –
   A heck of a feller
   A treat of a teller
   A million-volume version of a man.

   Boccacc-i-o's Decameron
   Is nothing to the likes of me.
   A Thousand and One Arabian Nights
   Are but a triviality
   And Proust is a slim slim volume
   And Tolstoy a trite little joke.
   I'm the Genie in the Bottle.
   I'm the guy you'd like to throttle
   I'm a never-ending sequel of a bloke!

I'm the Library of Alexandria!
I'm a desertful of Dead Sea Scrolls!
I'm a whole heap of hieroglyphics!
I'm the Greatest Story Ever Told!
I'm the soap of the soapiest opera!
I'm the Tale of a Tub at the turn of a tap!
I'm the Art of Diction!
I'm the Supreme Fiction!
I'm a multi-story carpark of a chap!

MR SENGUPTA *[to Soraya]*:
Supreme fiction indeed.
I'll give him a supreme fiction one of these days,

Excuse me if I mention
Excuse me if I dare
Excuse me but your husband
Has his head stuck in the air.
And what are all these stories?
And what are they to you?
(My dear)
What's the use of stories
That aren't even true?

HAROUN *[overhearing]*:
What's the use of stories that aren't even true?
What a terrible question!

Father, where do stories come from?
Everything comes from somewhere
So a story couldn't come out of thin air.
The river comes from the mountain . . .

RASHID:
  Correct!

HAROUN:
  The rain comes from the sky . . .

RASHID:
  Spot on!
  And the stories come from the Great Story Sea
  And I shall never drink it dry.
  I drink the warm story waters
  Then I feel full of steam.

HAROUN:
  Ridiculous!

MR SENGUPTA [*aside to Soraya*]:
  My car is waiting.
  Come with me my dear,
  My dearest.

RASHID:
  And the stories come bubbling out of me . . .

HAROUN:
  Any more of this nonsense and I'll scream!

RASHID [*speaking*]:
  The story water comes out of an invisible tap
      installed by one of the Water Genies.
  Of course you have to be a subscriber.

HAROUN:
  And how do you do that?

RASHID:

By a P2C2E – a Process Too Complicated To Explain.

How does a stroke of genius
Strike on the stroke of three?
By a P2C2.

HAROUN:

P2C2?

BOTH:

P2C2E!

RASIIID:

It's a complicated business
Which one day you will learn.
It's a wonder!
It's an enigma!
But you will have your turn
(My boy)
If I stand you a subscription
Will you do the same for me
For a P2C2.

HAROUN:

Me too see through.

BOTH:

The P2C2E!

RASHID:

Now why should your mother have written me a
    letter?
Why couldn't she have spoken herself?
Let's see:

'My dear Rashid, my husband as was,
You are only interested in pleasure
But a proper man would know
That life is a serious business.
You have your head in the clouds –'

HAROUN:

That's what Mr Sengupta always says.
That sounds like Mr Sengupta!

RASHID:

'And your feet off the ground.
Your brain is full of make-believe
So there is no room for facts.
Mr Sengupta has no imagination at all.
This is okay by me.'
Oh No.

    [Drops letter, which Haroun picks up.]

HAROUN:

'Tell Haroun I love him
But I can't help him any more.
I have to strike out now for a new life.
I have to slam the door.'

RASHID:

Eleven o'clock precisely.
She must have planned it all
To the last detail.

    *[Takes up clock and smashes it. Goes on
    rampage smashing clocks.]*

MRS SENGUPTA:
   They've gone. They've gone together.
   I knew there was something up.
   It was you neglecting your wife gave him the chance
   And he took it like the rat that he is! Oh! Oh!

HAROUN:
   That was *my* clock. Why did you smash my clock?

RASHID:
   What to do, son.
   What to say, where to go.
   This always telling stories
   This is the only work I know.

HAROUN:
   But what's the point of it?
   What's the use of stories that aren't even true?

   [Rashid hides his face and weeps.]

HAROUN:
   If I could catch those words I spoke
   And take them back again
   I'd pay whatever price it took
   Not to have seen your pain.

   To turn the clock back a minute or less
   To catch the word on the wing
   I'd pay whatever price it took
   Not to have done this thing.

   I hurt you then. I know it now.
   I knew it at the time.

But a word can strike like a criminal
And flee from the scene of the crime.

Return to the scene, O criminal word –
Isn't that what criminals do?
Return, return to the scene of the crime.
I have my dagger here for you.

Scene Two

ANNOUNCER:
Ladies and Gentlemen,
The moment you have all been waiting for –
The great Ocean of Notions himself,
The Shah of Blah,
The Supreme Fiction –
    *[Spoken in the manner of a TV sports
    announcer]*
Mr Rashid Khalifa!

    [Applause.]

CHORUS:
Tell us a story
Making it sentimental
And gentle
Or gory!

Tell us a story
Of caliphs and eunuchs and ogres
Or
Of Romans in tunics and togas
Shouting MEMENTO MORI!

Tell us a story
Of paynim knights and damozels
Or
Of fishnet tights and mam'selles
Inflammatory.

Tell us a story
Of the dragon, the hippogriff and the centaur
And other such mythological impedimenta
As are obligatory –
Tell us a Story
Now!
  [Pause.]
If you please!

RASHID:

Now let me see, in the Valley of Hum
In the days of who the devil was it . . .

CHORUS:

This opening is inauspicious. Please improve.

RASHID:

In the Valley of Hum in the days of Ha . . .

CHORUS:

This exposition is exiguous.
We have nothing to go on.
Give us some facts.

RASHID:

In the Ha of Hum . . .

CHORUS:

This is minimalism.

RASHID:
    Ho?! Hum?
    Ark. Ark.

CHORUS:
    Verging on subliminalism.
    You have exhausted our patience
    With these equivocations.
    Have some rotten eggs in return.

      [Crowd pelts Rashid.]

Scene Three

RASHID *[solus]*:
    Well, what's the use?
    I had it all once
    And now it seems I'm through
    But who cares? Who's there to care
    If I've run out of juice?
    I might as well put my head in a noose.
    What's the use of stories that aren't even true?

    Oh, it was all my imagination.
    I had one once
    And now it's flown into the blue.
    But who cares? I've lost the caring part of me,
    My instinct and my art.
    I'm just a flake.
    I might as well jump in the lake.
    What's the use of stories that aren't even true?

I'm done.
My wife thinks herself well shot of me,
I'm an embarrassment to my son.
I've lost the thread.
I've lost the plot of me.
I might as well be dead
And through.
What's the use of stories that aren't even true?

MRS SENGUPTA:
I tell you something, Mr Khalifa.
Independence is a beautiful thing.
No more Mrs Sengupta for me!
From today, call me Miss Oneeta only.
    [Sings her torch song, with diminishing
        confidence.]
I'm empowered
Bright as a frying pan that I myself
Have recently scoured.

I'm empowered!
The woman I once was
Oh, that bloody woman was perfectly obviously
A bloody coward.
Now I'm empowered
I'm not afraid to live alone.
I don't sit waiting by the phone
Nor do I cry myself to sleep
(Or not as much as I used to)
And – you know – my existence has not soured.
I'M EMPOWERED!
    [Bursts into tears.]
O! O! What is to become.

RASHID:
   What is to become indeed.
   What is to become of all of us.
   I've lost the gift of the gab
   And the strangest thing has happened to Haroun.
   He seems to have lost his powers of concentration.
   Eleven minutes is as long as he can last.
   After eleven, niente, nada, nix.

MRS SENGUPTA:
   It's his pussy-collar-jee.

RASHID:
   I see.

MRS SENGUPTA:
   You follow my drift.

RASHID:
   Well, no. Not your *drift*, as such.
   Explain please.

MRS SENGUPTA:
   His mother left at eleven o'clock precisely.
   That was when you broke all the clocks.
   It's pussy-collar-jee!

HAROUN [*overhearing*]:
   That isn't true.
   Or maybe it *is* true.
   I seem to stumble
   After eleven minutes
   And even when I count to eleven
   My mind begins to wander.
   What lies beyond eleven

Is wrapped in mystery.
I'm stuck in time like a broken clock.
I have no future.

　　[Enter two men.]

RASHID:
　Who are you?
　And why are you looking at me askance?

TWO MEN:
　We are two men in moustachios
　And yellow check pants.

RASHID:
　I see I'm in for the high-jump.
　Tell me what this mission means.
　Cut the crap and spill the beans.

TWO MEN:
　Supposing a teller of stories
　Got work from a powerful man
　To tell the public stories
　As only a storyteller can

　And this powerful man had a rival
　Who paid the old guy on the side
　To pretend to forget all his stories –

RASHID:
　It's not true!

TWO MEN:
　And the silly old story-teller went and lied
　And the powerful man grew angry
　'Cos the story-teller had taken a bung

So he sent out his trusted henchmen
To cut out the story-teller's tongue –

What a pity
What a horrible pity
What a horrible pity that would be!

RASHID:
I deny it all.
I *have* been indisposed of late
But at our next appointment
In the Valley of K
I shall be terrifico
Magnifico.
Splendifico.

TWO MEN:
Better you are
Better you are
Or out comes that tongue from your lying throat.
What a pity
What a horrible pity
What a horrible pity that would be.
    [Spoken]
And in case you think us incapable of such an
    outrage, here's one we prepared earlier.

[They hand Rashid a human tongue.]

HAROUN:
My fault again.
I started all this off.
What's the use of stories that aren't even true?
I asked the question

And it broke my father's heart.
And now it's up to me to put things right.
Something has to be done.
Something has to be done.
And the trouble is – I haven't a clue in my head.

Scene Four
On the Road

CHORUS:
    Get on the bus.
    Get on the bus.
    Get on the bus and come with us.
    Vegetables, goats and chickens
    Sacks of rice and what the dickens
    Leaking parcels, bags of rye
    Fling them in and pile them high –
    Get on the bus.

    Get on the bus.
    Get on the bus.
    Get on the bus and come with us.
    Gentlemen of many parts,
    Travelling salesmen, unravelling tarts,
    Hucksters, fixers, confidence trickers,
    Muckers, suckers, city slickers –
    Get on the bus.

    Unsavoury monks
    Get out of your bunks –
    Get on the bus.

Get on the bus
With us.

BUTT:

You seem a tip-top type, young man.
My goodname is Butt
Driver of the Number One
Super Express mail-coach
To the Valley of K.
At your service, sir!

HAROUN:

To the Valley of K?
Hey, if you mean what you say
And you really are at my service
Then there *is* something you can do.

BUTT:

It was a figure of speech
But but but
I shall stand by my figure of speech.
Butt's a straight man
Not a twister.
What's your wish
My young mister?

HAROUN:

Now let me see . . .
From the town of G
There runs a way
To the Valley of K . . .

BUTT:

Correct!

HAROUN:

    And from the Pass of H
    To the tunnel of I
    There's a hairpin bend . . .

BUTT:

    There are twenty bends
    And that's where many a journey ends.

HAROUN:

    But when you come through the tunnel
    To the Valley of K –
    Or so my father tells me –
    There's a view to take your breath away
    And no man can be sad
    – Or so says my dad –
    Who sees that view
    When the fields are gold
    The mountains silver
    And the sky is blue.
    Just give us two front seats
    And cheer my dad up with that view.

BUTT:

    But but but
    The hour is late.
    We'll never be there before dark.
    But but but
    So what – let's try.
    Let the sad dad have his day
    All aboard for the Valley of K!

Scene Five
To the Valley of K

CHORUS:
Driver, driver, not so fast.
Every moment could be our last.

BUTT:
The snow line! Icy patches ahead! Hurrah!

CHORUS:
If you try to rush or zoom
You are sure to meet your doom.

BUTT:
Crumbling road surface! Hurrah!

CHORUS:
All the dangerous overtakers
End up safe at undertakers.

BUTT:
Hairpin bends! Hurrah!

CHORUS:
Look out. Slow down. Don't be funny.
Life is precious. Cars cost money.

BUTT:
Danger of avalanches! Hurrah!

CHORUS:
If from speed you get your thrill
Take precaution – make your will.

BUTT:
Full speed ahead into the Valley of K! Hurrah!

CHORUS:
Aaagh!

> *[They enter the tunnel.]*

Scene Six
In the Dark

BUTT *[spoken, amplified, with reverberation]*:
Like I said, Tunnel.
At the far end, Valley of K.
Hours to sunset, one.
Time in tunnel, some moments only.
One view coming up.
Like I said, no problem.

> *[They emerge from the tunnel.]*

CHORUS:
Aaah!

Scene Seven
In the Valley of K

HAROUN:
So it was all true.
The fields are gold with saffron.

The mountains are silver with snow
And the skies are blue.

RASHID:

Thanks for fixing this up, son.
But I admit
I thought we were all fixed up good and proper.
Done for. Finito. Khattam-shud.

HAROUN:

Khattam-shud?
What was that story you used to tell?

RASHID:

Khattam-shud is the Arch-Enemy of all stories,
Even of language itself.
He is the Prince of Silence
And the Foe of Speech.

Everything ends.
Everything must come to an end.
Dreams end.
Stories end.
Life ends.
And so at the end of everything we use his name.
We say:
It is finished.
It is over.
Khattam-shud: The End.

HAROUN:

Khattam-shud.
This place is doing you good.
Your crazy stories are coming back.

CHORUS:
   Get on the bus.
   Get on the bus.
   Get on the bus and come with us.

Scene Eight
Meeting Mr Buttoo

SNOOTY BUTTOO:
   Mr Rashid
   Esteemed Mr Rashid –
   A legend comes to town:
   The Shah of Blah deigns to make his way
   To the Valley of K.
   A pleasure to meet you.
   The name is Buttoo.

HAROUN:
   Almost the same
   As the bus-driver's name.

BUTTOO:
   My dear young man, not at all the same.
   Bus-driver?
   Suffering Moses,
   Do I *look* the bus-driver type?
   Do you know to whom you speak?
   I am Snooty Buttoo!

HAROUN:
   Well, excuse *me* –

BUTTOO:
   Respected Mr Rashid,
   Bearers will carry your bags.
   And yours too, I suppose, young man.

HAROUN and RASHID:
   Soldiers everywhere
   And armoured cars
   And helmeted policemen
   Lounging outside the bars
   Burly men and surly men
   Wandering around –
   There's a sad feeling,
   A bad feeling
   In this town.

   You can smell it on the highway
   At night, when the trucks are gone
   And the moon is shining
   Bright as a silver piece
   You can smell it in the alleyways
   When the blinds are drawn
   And the flame of the nightlight
   Gutters in a pool of grease.

   Sleeping out on the rooftops
   Underneath the stars.
   Gunshots from the mountains.
   Gunshots from the bars.
   Fearful men and tearful men
   Stretched out on the ground –
   There's a sad feeling,

A bad feeling
In this town.

HAROUN:
How popular can Mr Buttoo be
If he needs all these soldiers to protect him?
And why should my father
Tell stories for his campaign?

BUTTOO:
Here is the swan-boat.
Tonight you stay as my guest
In the finest houseboat on the lake.
I trust it will not prove too humble
For a grandee like you.

Scene Nine
The Floating Gardens

RASHID:
You see, Haroun, you see –
The Floating Gardens.
They weave a floating mat of lotus root.
You can grow vegetables on the lake.
That is, if you *want* to.

HAROUN:
You sound sad, father.
Don't be sad.

BUTTOO:

Sad? Did someone say sad?
Surely the eminent story-teller
Is satisfied with all we have done for him?

RASHID:

Sir, I am more than satisfied.
This sadness is an affair of the heart.

BUTTOO:

Wife left you, did she?
Never mind.
There are plenty more fish in the sea.

HAROUN:

Fish? Did he say fish?
Is my mother a pomfret?
Is she a shark?
Why doesn't father bop this Buttoo on the nose?

RASHID:

But you must go a long long way
To find Angel Fish.
Those Angel Fish are few and far between.

HAROUN:

Never mind Angel Fish.
I can't even see to the tip of my –

RASHID *[spoken]*:

Phoo! Who made that smell?
Come on. Admit.

HAROUN:

    It is the mist.
    We seem to have rowed
    Into the Mist of Misery.
    It is the Misery makes the Mist.

BUTTOO:

    That boy is crazy for make-believe
    Like the folk of this foolish valley.
    My enemies tell bad stories about me
    And the ignorant people lap it up like milk.
    So I have turned to you, Mr Rashid.
    You shall tell happy stories
    You shall tell praising stories
    And the people will believe you
    And they will vote for me!
    All of the people will vote for me!!

    All the people will vote for me
    Whether they like or no –
    The muddy peasant with his ruddy wife,
    The butcher with his bloody knife,
    The nice boy on the way to school,
    The ice-boy with his ice-chopping tool,
    The master of the silver band,
    The lowly crematorium hand,
    All the people will vote for me
    Several times in a day.
    None of them will get away
    Until they vote for me!!

    All the people will vote for me
    Whether they like or no –

The laundress with her steamy vat,
The brothel madame and her cat,
The oily spiv with fancy wheels,
The transvestite in six-inch heels,
The chap in the chupatti flour,
The departed Parsee in the Vulture Tower –
All the people will vote for me
Several times in a day.
None of them will get away
Until they vote for me!!

HAROUN:

Funny how that harsh hot wind
Began to blow
As soon as Snooty Buttoo began to speak.
This lake is positively temperamental.
Perhaps we have come to the Moody Land.

The Moody Land, the Moody Land
I heard my father say
When people were happy in the Moody Land
The sun would turn the night to day.
But when the sun got on their nerves
My father said to me
An irritable night would fall
Full of mutterings and misery.

And if they were neither happy nor sad
But muddled and unsure
The colours would run in the Moody Land
And every outline became obscure.

Oh father, father, take my hand
And try the trick with me.

Let us spread some joy in the Moody Land
And clear the Mist of Misery.

RASHID:
My son, my son,
The Moody Land was only a story.

HAROUN:
Now I know how sad he is.
'Only a story' indeed!
The Shah of Blah would never have spoken like that
In the good old days.
And now the mist is getting worse.

[*Lightning, Thunder.*]

OARSMEN:
Oh Oh Oh, down we go!

HAROUN [*spoken*]:
Okay. Everybody listen.
Stop talking. This is very important.
Not a word. Zip the lips
On a count of one two three.
One!

(I must try to calm them down
Or we'll definitely drown.)

Two!

(I must calm myself as well
And not let Buttoo break the spell.)

Three!

Now the waves and wind are gone
But the mist is lingering on.
Father, father, help your son.
Think of the happiest times you can.
Think of happiness gone by.
Think your happiness across the sky!

[The mist disappears and the moon comes out.]

RASHID:
Now the sea is calm, and here's the moon.
You're a blinking good man
In a blinking tight spot.
Hats off to you, Haroun.

[They arrive at the houseboat.]

Scene Ten
On the Houseboat

BUTTOO:
Welcome to my houseboat,
The largest and best on the lake.
I have called it Arabian Nights Plus One
Because even in the Arabian Nights
You will never have a night like this.
For you, erudite Mr Rashid
Here is the peacock room,
And here on the shelves you will find
The entire collection of tales known as
The Ocean of the Streams of Story.

If ever you run out of material
You will find plenty here.

RASHID:

Run out? What are you saying?

BUTTOO:

Touchy touchy, Mr Rashid!
It was a joke only,
A passing lightness,
A cloud blown away on the breeze.
Of course we have the highest expectations
Of your performance tomorrow
And all the *praising* stories
That will redound to our credit.
Of course we have . . .
[*Spoken*] Don't we?
Now as for you, young man,
We have given you the turtle room.

HAROUN:

Thank you, it is very pleasant.

BUTTOO:

Very pleasant, indeed!
Inappropriate young person,
This is Arabian Nights Plus One.
'Very Pleasant' doesn't cover it at all.
Supermarvelloso, perhaps.
Incredibable, and wholly fanta*stick*!
All the best belongs to me!
Belongs to me!
Belongs to me!
The biggest vest!

The biggest treasure chest!
The biggest bathroom in the East or West!
Everything best belongs to me
By right!
Good night!

Scene Eleven
Changing bedrooms

> *Night music.*

RASHID:
It's no use.
I won't be able to tell my stories.
I'm finished, finished for good.
'Only praising tales' indeed.
I am the Ocean of Notions.
I am the Shah of –
Well, I'm not some office boy for Snooty Buttoo to
  boss about.
But what am I saying?
What if I get up on stage and have nothing to say?
They'll slice me in pieces.
They'll come and cut out my tongue.
It'll be up with me for good.
Finito. Khattam-shud!

Since you left me
Since you cleft my heart in two
Since you bereft me
There's nothing deft that I can do

I've no heft left
Since you tore the weft in two
Cleft my heart
Left me apart
From you.

Even my arias run out of rhymes.

HAROUN:
Still singing about my mother.

RASHID:
Who's there?

HAROUN:
It's me. I couldn't sleep.
I couldn't sleep on the turtle bed.
It's too weird.

RASHID:
That's funny. I've been having problems with this
    peacock.
I'd rather a turtle any night.
How do you feel about the bird?

HAROUN:
Definitely better.
A bird sounds okay.

RASHID:
Well then, let's swap.
Now get some sleep, young man.

Scene Twelve
The Story Tap

IFF:
Do this. Do that.
Put it in. Take it out.
Rush job. Hush-hush job.
Never mind my workload.

Hot tap. Cold tap.
Story tap. Disconnect.
Cash job. On account.
On the never-never.

Never so much as a by-your-leave.
Never a thought for me sir.
Disconnect my story tap
At the hour of three sir.

Do this. Do that.
Put it in. Take it –
      [Interrupting himself]
And on top of it all, where's my disconnecting tool?
Who's pinched it? Where are you?
No kidding. Well, enough's enough.
Party's over. Fair's fair.
GIVE IT BACK.

HAROUN:
No.

IFF:

The Disconnector. Hand it over.
Return to sender.
Yield. Surrender.

HAROUN:

You're not getting it back
Until you tell me what you are doing here.
Are you a burglar?
Shall I call the cops?

IFF:

Mission impossible to divulge.
Top secret, classified. Eyes only info.
Zip the lips
Or you've had your chips.

HAROUN:

Very well. Then I'll wake my father.

IFF:

No. No adults.
Rules and regulations.
No parents or other close relations.

HAROUN:

I'm waiting for some explanations.

IFF:

I am the Water Genie Iff
From the Ocean of the Streams of Story.
You may think as a boy you're adorable.
I call you deplorable.

HAROUN:
Are you really one of those genies
My father told me about?

IFF:
Supplier of Story Water from the Great Story Sea.
Precisely the same. No other. It is me.
Or rather it is I.
I is it.
Hence this visit.
I regret to report
The gentleman your father
No longer requires the service.
He has discontinued narrative activities
Thrown in the towel
Told his last story
To its last vowel.
And hence my presence
For the purpose of disconnection of his story tap –
To which end, kindly return my tool.

HAROUN:
Not so fast.
I don't believe you.
How did he send the message?
I've been with him almost all the time.

IFF:
He sent it by the usual means –
A P2C2E.

HAROUN:
And what is that?

IFF:

    Obvious.
    It's a Process Too Complicated To Explain.

    How does the Story Water
    Come from the Story Sea
    By a P2C2
    P2C2
    P2C2E!

    It's a most mysterious business
    And hard to deconstruct.
    It's a riddle.
    It's a conundrum.
    But it's utterly ineluct-
    able
    If you think of my department
    You can think straight through to me
    By a P2C2.

HAROUN:

    No! Not he too!

BOTH:

    A P2C2E!

IFF:

    Something to do with thought-beams.
    We listened to your father's thoughts –

HAROUN:

    And you got the wrong end of the stick
    My father has definitely not given up.

IFF:

Well, those are my orders.
If you have any queries
Please address them to:
P2C2E House
Gup City
Kahani.

HAROUN:

Mr Iff, take me at once to Gup City!

IFF:

Oh, what a pity.
Gup City is banned, off limits, strictly restricted.

HAROUN:

In that case you'll have to go back without *this*
And see how they like *that*.

IFF:

Okay, I give in.
You've got me bang to rights.
But if we're going, let's go now.

HAROUN:

You mean – now?

IFF:

Now means now.

If you have something to do
Do it now.
Thinking of tying a shoe?
Tie it now.
Don't wait to slip

And trip on the street
– That is complete-
ly insane.
Think what advantage you gain
Doing it now.

If you have somewhere to go
Go there now.
Though it is far as the crow
Flies, fly now.
Don't wait to pack
A rucksack or two.
That is the u-
sual way.
Trust your first impulse and say:
I'll go there now.

So, pick a bird.

HAROUN:
The only bird around here
Is a sort of wooden peacock.

IFF:
Foolish thieflet,
A person may choose what he cannot see.
A person may mention a bird's name
Even if that creature is not present and correct.
A woodpecker, for instance, or a whinchat,
A wheatear, a waxwing or a wattlebird,
A whimbrel, a whistler or a wagtail,
A wigeon, a wedgebill or a weebill,
A whipbird, a warbler or a whiteye,
A whippoorwill, or a white-winged wydah –

All these exist, but there is more to come.
For a person may select.
A flying creature of his own invention –
A winged horse or a flying turtle,
An airborne whale or an aeromouse.
To give a thing a name, a label, a handle,
To pluck it out of the Place of Namelessness,
In short to identify it –
Well, that's a way of bringing
The said thing into being –
Or, in this case,
The said bird or Imaginary Flying Organism.
    [Spoken]
So, pick a bird.

Think of all the birds you can,
Of all the winged creatures
Known and unknown to man.

HAROUN:
I see a lion with a human head
And curly beard and hairy wings,
I see a monkey fly from tree to tree,
Angels and flying saucers, stranger things
Than ever I've heard said.

I see a school of levitating fish
Gulping the air and heading for the sky
And all these birds which seem to turn to me
And offer me the wings to fly –
Fly where my heart could wish

And offer me the wings to fly
Go heading for the open sky

Fly where my heart could wish.
Swim like a bird.
Fly like a fish.
Go heading for the open sky.

So, I'll chose that one –
The one with the funny crest.

IFF:
So, it's the Hoopoe for us.
A significant choice!

[*Throws miniature Hoopoe out of window.*]

HAROUN:
What was *that* for?

IFF:
Wait and see.

[*A huge Hoopoe arrives.*]

And off we go!

Scene Thirteen
Flying to the Moon

HAROUN:
That's odd, that floating feeling.
Just like on the mail coach ride.
And this Hoopoe with its feathers
Reminds me quite a bit of old Butt.
Butt with his quiff of hair.

Butt's hair seemed feathery
And these feathers seem hairy.
No bird could fly so fast.
Is this a machine?

BUTT THE HOOPOE:
But if I was?
Do you have some objection to machines?
But but but
You entrusted your life to me –
Am I not worthy of a little respect?
A machine
Is entitled to some self-esteem
Or so it seems
To me.

HAROUN:
You seem to be reading my mind.

BUTT:
But but but certainly.
And I am speaking to you by telepathy.

HAROUN:
And how do you do that?

BUTT and IFF:
By a P2C2E.

How does a hurtling hoopoe
Speak by telepath-ee?

ALL:
By a P2C2
P2C2
P2C2E!

BUTT:
See there.
That is the second moon of Earth –
Kahani.

HAROUN:
But but but
How can the earth have a second moon?
It would have been discovered!

BUTT:
Speed, speed –
It is the speed of the moon
Kahani.

Speed of the moon
Speed of the moon
Necessary
Needful speed

Shine like a spoon
Fly like a steed
Luminary
Lunar speed

Speed that conceals
Speed that reveals
Speed of hand and foot and thigh
Voom! Varoom!

Away we zoom!
Speed of a glance or a glint in the eye

Speed of the moon
Speed of the moon
Necessary
Needful speed.

IFF and BUTT:
Be heedful Haroun
Of the speed of the moon
Heedful of the needful speed
Heedful of the needful speed.

> *[Rushing towards them is a sparkling and*
> *seemingly infinite expanse of water.]*

IFF:
The Ocean of the Streams of Story –
Wasn't it worth travelling
So far and fast to see?

BUTT:
Three two one zero!

> *[They land on the Moon Kahani.]*

Scene Fourteen
Wishwater

HAROUN:

    It's a trick.

    There's no Gup City here –

    No point in being here at all.

IFF:

    Hold your horses.

    Cool down.

    Keep your hair on.

    Everything will be explained.

HAROUN:

    But this is the Middle of Nowhere!

IFF:

    This is the Deep North of Kahani

    And here we may find Wishwater.

BUTT:

    Look for the brightest patches of water.

    That is wishwater.

    Use it properly

    And you can make a wish come true.

IFF:

    Wish for your father, Haroun,

    And maybe you can make this problem disappear

    And we can all go home.

HAROUN:

Oh very well.
Though I should have liked to see Gup City too.

IFF:

Tip top type!
Prince among men!
And hey presto – wishwater ahoy.

> *[Iff fills a bottle with wishwater and hands it to Haroun.]*

IFF and BUTT:

Drink the water.
The harder you wish
The better it will work.
Your heart's desire
Will be as good as yours.
So – down the hatch!

HAROUN:

I wish – what will I wish?
My wishes fly before me
Like a school of flying fish.

I wish my father well . . .
I wish him all the happiness of heart
And art
To tell . . .
To tell my mother to come home again!
No, that's not right.
Not quite.

I wish – what will I wish?
My wishes fly before me
Like a school of flying fish.

I see my father pleading
Saying: do this one thing for me . . .
What thing?
What can that be?
Maybe my father telling stories every day
Made my mother run away.
I wish she would come back.
No . . . that's a different track . . .

I wish – what would I wish?
My wishes fly before me
Like a school of flying fish –
Flashing
Dashing
Disappearing
Like a school of flying fish.

IFF:
Eleven minutes –
Just eleven minutes and his concentration goes
Ka-bam, ka-blooey, ka-put.

HAROUN:
I know.
I have failed.

BUTT:
Wishes are not such easy things.
Don't bully the boy.
You, Mister Iff, are upset

Because of your own mistake,
Because we must go to Gup City after all
And there will be harsh words,
Harsh words and hot water for you.
Stop taking it out on the boy.

IFF:

But but but . . .
Okay Okay Okay,
Gup City it is.
Unless of course
You'd like to hand over the Disconnecting Tool
And call the whole thing off.

[Haroun shakes his head miserably.]

BUTT:

But but but
You're still bullying the boy.
Cheer him up man
Cheer him up.
Give him a happy story to drink.

HAROUN:

Not another drink.
What are you going to make me fail at now?

IFF:

Cheer up, Haroun,
And look at all the colours of the sea.
It is a liquid tapestry
Of breathtaking complexity.
This is the Ocean of the Streams of Story.
Every tale that has been told is here

And every tale that has yet to be invented
And if you're very careful
You can dip a cup into the ocean
And fill it with a single story –
A single pure stream of story
Like so.
Go on now. Knock it back.
Guaranteed to make you feel
A-number-one.

> *[Haroun takes a cup, dips into the sea, and drinks a story.]*

Scene Fifteen
The Story He Drank

PRINCESS:
An outlandish knight from the north country came
And he came for to rescue me
And the four-headed lion did shake its mane
Most grisly for to see.

Oh have you seen the noble knight
And have you heard his tune?
It is the fairest knight in the land
And his name it is Sir Haroun.

Oh yes, I've seen the noble knight
A-pricking o'er the plane
And the sun did on his helmet shine
As on a mountain after the rain.

HAROUN:

Let down, let down your flaxen hair
And I shall climb to thee
And I shall slay your jailer bold
And I shall your rescuer be.

PRINCESS:

And so I let down my flaxen hair
And he began to climb
But then . . . I felt a hairy leg

And EEK it was a spider all the time!

Eek my dearest – you have into a spider turned!

[Attacks Haroun with knife.]

Scene Sixteen
Flying to Gup City

IFF:

Wake up, snap out of it.
Let's have you.
What happened?
Did you save the Princess?

HAROUN:

I was saving her.
But then I turned into a spider.

IFF:

Turned into a spider
In a Princess Rescue Story?

I can't believe it.
Never in all my born days.

HAROUN:
I'm glad to hear it
Because I was thinking
That it wasn't the most brilliant way
To cheer me up.

BUTT:
It's pollution.
Something or someone has been putting filth
Into the Ocean of the Streams of Story.
If the stories get polluted they go wrong.

IFF:
And if the pollution has come as far as the Deep
   North
Then Gup City could be close to crisis.

BUTT:
Top speed ahead!

BUTT and IFF:
This could mean war!

HAROUN:
War with whom?

BUTT:
With the Land of Chup
On the dark side of Kahani.
This looks like the doing of the leader of the
   Chupwalas –
The Cultmaster of Bezaban himself.

HAROUN:
And who is that?

IFF and BUTT:
His name is Khattam-Shud.

HAROUN:
Too many fancy notions
Are turning out to be true.
Tell me more about Khattam-Shud.

IFF:
Khattam-Shud is the arch-enemy of all stories,
Even of Language itself.
He is the Prince of Silence
And the Foe of Speech.

HAROUN:
Exactly what my father told me.

IFF and BUTT:
On the far side of the moon
Darker than the deepest wood
In a permanence of gloom
Lives the Master Khattam-Shud.

And the dark Chupwalas go
Fearful of his least command
And their sombre legions know
Deeds done by his dreadful hand.

Everything must have an end,
Die, decay and decompose.
Friendship falter, falter friend.
Shorn the shape the shadow shows.

In the shadow of the moon
Darker than the deepest wood
You shall know, if you go, Haroun,
Khattam-Shud, Khattam-Shud –

You shall know
If you shall go
Khattam-Shud
Khattam-Shud.

HAROUN:
Look at all the birds.
The sky is filling up with birds.

IFF:
Something serious has happened.
All units have been called back to base.

HAROUN:
Listen.
Listen to the beating of their wings.
Listen to the song of the birds.

CHORUS OF BIRDS:
Halcyon blue
Halcyon blue
We're flying through the halcyon blue
On a thermal
On a high
Like mackerel in a mackerel sky.

Heaviside Layer
Heaviside Layer
We're flying through the Heaviside Layer
On a cyclone

Cycling near
Cycling home through the exosphere.

Bats have wings
And sprats have wings
And pterodactyls have similar things
To bring them through
The tropopause
And pare their nails and clip their claws.

Halcyon blue
Halcyon blue
We're flying home through the halcyon blue
On a thermal
On a high
Like mackerel in a mackerel sky.

HAROUN:
What's that?

BUTT:
A floating gardener of course.

> [Mali appears.]

Look – he floats, he runs, he hops.
No problem.

MALI:
Who are you, stranger?

HAROUN:
I am Haroun Khalifa
From the sad city of Alifbay.

MALI:
I am Mali,
Floating Gardener First Class.

HAROUN:
Please
What does a floating gardener do?

MALI:
Untwisting twisted story streams.
Also unlooping same.
Weeding. In short: gardening.

BUTT and MALI:
Think of the Ocean as a head of hair.
The Story Streams are floating everywhere
As a thick mane is full of flowing strands
And you can run the stories through your hands.
Think of that hair growing longer every day
Thicker and knottier, tangled every way.
It needs a brush, conditioner, shampoo.
That's what a floating gardener has to do.

[Another squadron of birds passes.]

BIRDS:
Halcyon blue
Halcyon blue
We're flying through the halcyon blue
On a thermal
On a high
Like mackerel in a mackerel sky.

[Plentimaw fish arrive.]

BAGHA:

Hurry hurry, don't be late.

GOOPY:

Ocean's ailing. Cure can't wait.

HAROUN:

So there really *are* Plentimaw Fish in the Sea
Just as Snooty Buttoo said.
Excuse me,
Are you quite well?

BAGHA:

All this bad taste! Too much dirt!

GOOPY:

Swimming in the Ocean starts to hurt.

BAGHA:

Call me Bagha. This is Goopy.

GOOPY:

Excuse our rudeness. We feel droopy.

BAGHA and GOOPY:

Eyes feel rheumy. Throat feels sore.
When we're better we'll talk more.
Things are worse than we've ever known.
And the worst place is down in our Old Zone.

IFF:

What? What?
If the Old Zone is polluted
Then the Source of all Stories is poisoned
And if the source is poisoned

What will happen to the Ocean, to us all?
We have ignored it far too long
And now we pay the price.

BUTT [*spoken, amplified*]:
Hold on to hats.
Hitting the brake now.
Gup City ahead.
Record time!
Va-va-va-voom!
No-o-o problem!

[*They land in Gup City.*]

Scene Seventeen
War is Declared

CHORUS:
Now the lagoon is blue.
Now the lagoon is green.
And now the lagoon is strawberry jelly
And something in between.

Now the lagoon is damask grey
And now an amber silk,
And now the lagoon is a purple velvet
Dipped in a bath of asses' milk.

Stare in the depths of the water.
Stare in the depth, Haroun.
This is the biggest kaleidoscope
On the bright side of the moon.

These are the colours of thought.
These are the colours of dreams.
These are the colours of storylines.
These are the story streams.

Now the lagoon is red.
Now the lagoon is blue.
Now the lagoon is everything
Everything a lagoon should be –
Topaz, quartz, chalcedony –
Doing everything a lagoon should do,
Everything, Haroun, for you.

> *[The crowd bustling about.*
> *General Kitab appears and the crowd falls*
> *silent.]*

GENERAL KITAB:
Words fail the king.
He cannot speak to you.

CHORUS:
Words fail his Majesty?
This is most unusual.

GENERAL KITAB:
You tell them, Prince Bolo.
> *[Weeps.]*

PRINCE BOLO:
They have seized her!
They have seized the Princess Batcheat
My bride to be.
The servants of the Cultmaster
Khattam-Shud . . .

CHORUS [*softly*]:
  Khattam-Shud.

BOLO:
  Have made off with my future wife.
  Churls, varlets, dastards, hounds!
  By gum, they will pay for this!
  Will they not pay for this, General Kitab?
  Will they not pay through the nose for this?

GENERAL KITAB:
  My liege, it is the most blasted business.
  The Princess is now a prisoner
  In the citadel of Chup,
  The ice-castle of Khattam-Shud.

CHORUS [*softly*]:
  Khattam-Shud.

GENERAL KITAB:
  We have sent messages
  To the Cultmaster Khattam-Shud –

CHORUS [*softly*]:
  Khattam-Shud.

GENERAL KITAB:
  Oh *will* you stop interrupting?

  We have sent messages
  Concerning the vile poison being injected
  Into the Ocean of the Streams of Story
  And the abduction of the Princess.
  We demanded that he stop the pollution
  And return the King's daughter within seven hours.

Neither demand was met
And I have to inform you
That a state of war now exists
Between the lands of Gup and Chup.

[*Silence.*]

I said a state of war now exists
Between the lands of Gup and Chup.

[*Silence.*]

I must say.
You don't seem very interested.

CHORUS:
You told us not to interrupt you
And we obeyed to the letter.

GENERAL KITAB:
My dear friends
I seem to have offended you.
You must forgive a military man
His crusty old ways.

CHORUS:
It is never necessary or polite
To raise one's voice among friends.

GENERAL KITAB:
Oh, I *have* offended you.
Accept my most abject apologies.
Forgiveness, forgiveness
Forgiveness is all I ask.
Forgive me, my friends,

My failure to transcend
The limitations of my social class.

CHORUS:
Forgiveness, forgiveness
Forgiveness is all he asks.
For failure to transcend
The limitations of his social class.

GENERAL KITAB:
Forgive me, my friends,
My failure to transcend
The limitations of my social class.

CHORUS [*still seemingly offended*]:
Very well. Go back to what you were saying.

GENERAL KITAB:
I said I have to inform you
That a state of war now exists
Between the lands of Gup and Chup.

CHORUS [*after a split second, with amazing volume*]:
War! War! War! War!
War between the lands of Chup and Gup!
War between the lands of Gup and Chup!
A battle to the death!
A battle to the dying breath!
A struggle for the triumph of the forces of the Good!
A struggle for the overthrow of
    [*whispered*]
Khattam-Shud!

GENERAL KITAB *[spoken]*:
    That's exactly what I had in –

CHORUS:
    War! War! War! War!
    War between the lands of Chup and Gup!
    War between the lands of Gup and Chup!
    The armies of the night
    Are absolutely frightful.
    They are poisoning the Ocean like a poison of the
        blood
    And the frightfullest of all of them is
        [Pianissimo]
    Khattam-Shud!
        [Fortissimo]
    Khattam-Shud!

End of Act One

ACT TWO

Scene One
Rescue the Princess!

> *Outside the Palace, exactly as before. Chorus and singers frozen in the same positions.*

CHORUS:
  Khattam-Shud!

GENERAL KITAB:
  And now, herald, let my word go forth.
  Bring the spy before the people!

FIRST HERALD:
  Bring the spy before the treacle!

SECOND HERALD:
  Bring the pie before the treacle!

THIRD HERALD:
  Fling the pie before the treacle!

HAROUN:
  Fling the pie before the treacle?
  This could get messy?

GENERAL KITAB:
  You are right.
  Officer, bring the spy before the people.

> *[Footsteps approaching. Rashid is brought on with a sack over his head.]*

HAROUN:

That looks like *my* dad.
It *is* my dad.

RASHID:

Sir, there seems to be some mistake.
I am just a story-teller
And a long-time subscriber
To your story-water service.

CHORUS:

One of our own subscribers
And he has betrayed us!
Caught spying in the Twilight Strip.

HAROUN:

He's not a spy.
He's my father.

RASHID:

Haroun!

HAROUN:

And the only thing wrong with him
Is that he's lost the gift of the gab.

RASHID:

That's right, my son,
Tell everyone.
Broadcast it to the whole world.
Don't mind *my* feelings.
I'm just a humble story-teller
Who bit off more than he could chew.

I became over-extended
And now my story's ended.
　　[Weeps.]
It's so discouraging.

CHORUS:
　Aaah!

PRINCE BOLO:
　Tell us your story.
　I love a good story –
　Especially if *I* come into it.
　Tell us a Prince Bolo story.

RASHID:
　Oh very well then.

　It was like a dream.
　It *was* a dream.
　I fell asleep
　And I flew to the Twilight Strip.
　It was dark and the trees were dripping.

PRINCE BOLO:
　How utterly gripping!

RASHID:
　And there was the whole Chupwala Army
　Encamped in their black tents
　In fanatical silence.

PRINCE BOLO:
　Those black tents
　Are making *me* tense –
　Go on.

RASHID:
  I made my way
  Among those dull pavilions
  Among those millions of scullions
  Scouring their skillets
  Outside their billets
  When suddenly
  I heard the sound
  Of a young woman singing.

PRINCE BOLO:
  How wonderful!

RASHID:
  It was without doubt
  One of the most appalling experiences of my life –
  A voice like a parakeet
  In heat –
  Like so:
      [He imitates the voice]
  'An outlandish knight from the North Country
      came . . .'

CHORUS:
  Batcheat!
  He has heard the Princess Batcheat!

PRINCE BOLO:
  Princess Batcheat,
  My love, my bride to be!
  So this is a Prince Bolo story after all.
  Proceed, pronounce, for pity's sake.

RASHID:

    No sooner had the princess and her handmaidens
    Come into view
    Than a posse of Chupwalas
    Leapt from the bushes
    And bagged the lot of them
    Kicking and screaming.

PRINCE BOLO:

    And you did nothing?
    You did nothing to save them?

RASHID:

    Me? I did nothing?
    You mistake your man . . .
    Ahem . . . I, ah, I . . .

PRINCE BOLO:

    Well then . . .

RASHID:

    Sire, swift as a sunbeam
    I surveyed my situation.
    It was insupportable.
    An unspeakable peril.
    Not only was I unarmed and in my nightshirt.
    I was also outnumbered twenty-five to one.

PRINCE BOLO:

    Those odds are trifling.

RASHID:

    Exactly what I thought
    Until I heard something
    That made my blood run cold –

So cold, I decided
There was not a moment to lose.
I must seek help at once.
Prince Bolo, sire,
Are you sitting down?

PRINCE BOLO:
Of course not, I –

RASHID:
Be prepared for the worst.
As the Chupwala soldiers
Hauled the Princess away
Kicking and screaming
I heard one say:
'The great Feast of the Idol Bezaban
Is coming soon.
Let us offer this Guppee Princess
As a sacrifice.
Let us stitch up her lips
And sacrifice her to Bezaban.'

PRINCE BOLO:
Now there is not a second to lose!
Assemble the armed forces –
All the Pages,
Every Chapter,
Every Volume.
To war! To war!
For Batcheat, only Batcheat!

GENERAL KITAB:
For Batcheat and the Ocean!

RASHID:
　Sire, I shall lead you to the Chupwala tents.

HAROUN:
　I'm coming too.

RASHID:
　No, son.
　This could be dangerous.

HAROUN:
　All the more reason for sticking together.

　It's a Princess Rescue Story.
　It's a deed of derring-do.
　It's a case of death or glory.
　A priori
　It's my cue.

RASHID:
　Though the upshot may be gory
　We shall have to see it through.
　Though the story may be hoary
　A priori
　It's our cue.

CHORUS:
　It's a well-known category
　It's a tale that's tried and truc.
　It's a Princess Rescue Story
　A priori
　It's our cue.

Scene Two
To the Twilight Strip

BAGHA:
Saving Batcheat! What a notion.

GOOPY:
What matters now is to save the Ocean.

BAGHA:
That's the plan to set in motion.

GOOPY:
Find the source of the poison potion.

BAGHA and GOOPY:
The Ocean's the important thing.
Worth more than the daughter of any king.

HAROUN:
Sounds like mutinous talk to me.

BAGHA and GOOPY:
What's a Mutinus? Who he be?

HAROUN:
What a chattering, clattering, quarrelling crew
Sailing through the halcyon blue –
Floating gardeners, Pages, Barge-birds,
Plentimaw Fish
Plentimaw Fish
Plentimaw Fish in the Story Sea.

CHORUS:
　Chatter chatter chatter
　What's the matter if we chatter
　If we chatter chatter chatter on our way?
　Chatter chatter chatter all day?
　What's the matter with our patter
　With the clatter of our scattergun
　Rattling
　Battling
　Fray?

HAROUN:
　You'll give the game away!

CHORUS:
　Better to give
　Better to live
　Giving the game away.

HAROUN:
　What an absurd armada!
　How can we ever succeed?
　There isn't even any light
　To see the enemy by.
　We're on a suicide mission.
　Batcheat will perish
　And the Ocean will be ruined for ever.

BUTT:
　But but but
　Don't be depressed.
　You're suffering from Heart Shadow.
　Everyone gets it
　As they approach the Twilight Strip

Heart Shadow –
The night is brushing you
Brushing like a raven's wing
A fearful thing
To feel.

Heart Shadow –
The wind is rushing through
Rushing like a swollen stream
And yet it seems
Unreal.

MALI:
It feels like a memory
Buried somewhere beneath the snow.
It feels like a memory
Of something somehow lost long ago.

Heart Shadow –

MALI, IFF and BUTT:
That loss is crushing you
Crushing you before you start
Making you lose heart –
Heart Shadow.
You're feeling Heart Shadow.

[They land on the Twilight Strip.]

CHORUS:
Hush for a moment.
This is the Twilight Strip.

On these twilit shores
No birds sing.

No wind blows.
No voice speaks.
Feet falling on the shingle
Fall silently.

The air smells stale
And stenchy.
The bushes cluster around
And leafless trees
Like sallow ghosts.
All is still and all is cold.

The darkness is biding its time.

RASHID:
    The further they lure us
    Into the darkness
    The better for them.
    And they know we will come
    Because they are holding Batcheat.

HAROUN:
    I thought that Love
    Was supposed to conquer all
    But it seems that Love
    Makes monkeys of us –
    Makes mincemeat of the lot of us.

PRINCE BOLO:
    Storyteller
    Now is the hour
    When you must lead us to the tents of the
        Chupwalas.

Great matters are afoot.
We must save the Princess.

HAROUN:
Yes, father, you must help save the Princess
And I
I shall go down to the Old Zone
And I shall try to save the Sea of Stories.

RASHID:
To save the Sea of Stories singlehanded!
There's more to you, Haroun Khalifa,
Than meets the blinking eye.

HAROUN:
There's not a moment to lose.
The sea is dying even as we speak.
The sea is dying
And all the stories will be coming to an end.

RASHID:
Good luck, son.
Good luck, Haroun,
My pride and joy!

Oh, I feel as if I'd lost the plot entirely.

Scene Three
On the Way to the South Pole

IFF, BUTT and MALI:
Speed of the moon
Speed of the moon

Necessary
Needful speed

Shine like a spoon
Fly like a steed
Luminary
Lunar speed, etc.

HAROUN:
It's getting even colder
And the waters are losing their colour.

BAGHA and GOOPY:
We're going the right way! We can tell!
Before it was filthy! Now it's Hell!

HAROUN [*to* MALI]:
Does the poison hurt your feet?

MALI:
Poison?
A little poison? Bah!
A little acid? Pah!
I'm a tough old bird.
It won't stop me.

You can stop a cheque.
You can stop a leak or three.
You can stop traffic, but
You can't stop me.

HAROUN:
Nobody wants to.
We're out to stop the Cultmaster
Khattam-shud.

IFF:

> If the source of the Sea of Stories
> Is at the South Pole
> That's where Khattam-Shud will be.

HAROUN:

> To the South Pole.
> To the South Pole.

BUTT:

> Full speed ahead to the South Pole.

BAGHA and GOOPY:

> Never thought it would be so bad.
> We have failed you. We feel sad.
> I feel terrible. She feels worse.
> We can hardly speak in verse.

HAROUN:

> Stay here and keep watch.
> Goodbye.

> The water is growing thicker.
> It's like looking into molasses
> Through dark glasses.

MALI:

> These are the waters of neglect.
> These are the seas of disgrace.
> Give me a year and I expect
> I could clean this place.

HAROUN:

> But we haven't got a year.
> We haven't a moment to waste.

MALI:

I'll go ahead and I will clear
A channel through.

You can stop a cheque.
You can stop a leak or three.
You can stop traffic but
You can't stop me.

You can't stop me
(I said)
You can't stop – aaagh!

CHORUS:

Heh, heh, heh, heh.

[Hissing sound.]

HAROUN:

Mali. Mali! Where are you? Mali?

CHORUS:

Sss.

BUTT:

It is the Web of the Night.
We are caught in the Web of the Night.
And the Web will grip you harder
The harder you fight.

IFF:

It's no use.
It's no use.
Khattam-shud
Has cooked our goose.

HAROUN:

So we're prisoners already?
Some hero *I* turned out to be!

Scene Four
'They were being pulled slowly forwards'

IFF:

Up the creek
Pretty pickle
Had our chips is what I say.

BUTT:

Woe is us!
Alack-a-day!

IFF and BUTT:

Ai-ai-ai
Ai-ai-ai
It's zap, bam, phut, finito for us all.

HAROUN:

You're a fine pair of companions.
Pull yourselves together.

BUTT:

How can we pull ourselves anywhere
When we are being pulled in the Web of Night?

IFF:

Look down
Look down at the Ocean.

HAROUN:

It is as cold as death.

IFF:

Look at it now.
Look at it now.
The oldest stories ever made –
Look at them now.
We let them rot.
We abandoned them
And now they are utterly spoilt.

> *[The Web of Night is removed. They are
> surrounded by Chupwalas.]*

HAROUN:

We have stopped.
We must be on the edge
Of Perpetual Darkness.
They are taking us to the flagship
Of Khattam-Shud.

CHUPWALAS:

Sss! Sss! Sss!

> *[They are led on to the ship.]*

BUTT:

But but but
You must not take that –
That's my brain!

> *[The Chupwalas remove Butt's brain.]*

HAROUN:

Oh Hoopoe
I'm sorry I ever criticized you.
You're the bravest and best machine that ever was.
I'll get back your brain for you.

Oh brave machine
Now it's too late to tell you what you mean
To me
To say what might have been
What moments on this flight have been
With your machinery –

Oh brave machine
Now it's too late to tell you what you mean
To me
And now this night has been
The chance to put things right has been
Lost, all at sea
For you, for me,
With your machinery.

IFF:

Here, a little emergency something.
Maybe you'll get a chance to use it.

HAROUN:

What is it?

IFF:

Bite the end off
And it will give you two full minutes of light.

It's called a Bite-a-Lite.
Hide it under your tongue. Shh!

   [Haroun pockets the Bite-a-Lite.]

HAROUN:
   Look, it's a factory ship
   And those must be the poison tanks
   And yet it all seems
   Shadowy
   As if the whole thing were made of shadows.

POISON MACHINES:
   Oop-a-doop, boop.
   Oop-a-doop, boop.

   [Enter Khattam-shud.]

HAROUN:
   And who is this skinny, scrawny,
   Measly, weaselly, snivelling clerical type?
   Can this be the terrible Cultmaster himself
   Or could it be his shadow?
   He reminds me of someone.

KHATTAM-SHUD:
   Spies. What a melodrama.
   A Water Genie from Gup City
   And a young fellow from *down there*
   If I am not mistaken.

HAROUN:
   I know him.
   I've met him somewhere before.

KHATTAM-SHUD:
    What brought you here, young man?
    Stories, I suppose.
    Well, look where stories have landed you now.
    What started up as stories
    Has ended up as spying
    And you know what happens to spies, don't you?

    Excuse me if I mention
    Excuse me if I dare
    Excuse me but this young man
    Has his head right in the air.
    What started out with stories
    Has got him in a stew –
    Young man!
    What's the use of stories
    That aren't even true?

HAROUN:
    I know. You're him.
    You're Mr Sengupta and you stole my mother.

IFF:
    Haroun, lad, it's not the same guy.
    This is the Cultmaster of Bezaban, Khattam-Shud.

HAROUN:
    But I thought he was back in his Citadel!

KHATTAM-SHUD:
    He is. I am.
    That is, I am his shadow.
    We've split in two
    So I can poison the Ocean *here*

And defeat the Guppies *there*.
Body there. Shadow here.
No problem.
Heh-heh-heh.

Come, young Haroun,
And let me show you my poison-blenders.
We need all the poisons we can make
For every story to be ruined in a different way.
And I have discovered
That for every story there is an anti-story.
Put the two together
And they cancel each other out.
Every day we release new poisons.
Soon, now, soon
The Ocean will be dead –
Cold and dead –
And my victory will be complete.

HAROUN:
But why do you hate stories so much?
Stories are fun.

KHATTAM-SHUD:
Foolish child,
The world is not for fun.
The world is for controlling.
Inside every single story
There lies a world, a story world,
That I cannot rule at all.
Beyond my control!
Can you imagine it?

Can you imagine what that means to me?
It spoils everything!

[Mali is heard whistling.]

KHATTAM-SHUD:
What was that?
I gave the strictest instructions
Nobody should ever whistle.

VOICE OF MALI:
You can chop a flower-bush
You can chop a tree
You can chop liver but
You can't chop me.

KHATTAM-SHUD:
Intruder. Intruder alert!

HAROUN:
Hooray, Mali!

VOICE OF MALI:
You can chop and change
You can chop in ka-ra-tee
You can chop suey but
You can't chop me
(I said)
You can't chop me.

KHATTAM-SHUD:
Switch on the darkness!

[Blackout.]

HAROUN:

Come on now Haroun –
It's your turn now or never.

KHATTAM-SHUD:

This is control.
This is control.
Kill all the intruders.
Kill all the intruders.

HAROUN:

Let's see what a Bite-a-Lite can do.

> [*Brilliant light. Groaning and shrieking of Chupwalas.*]

Now if I just grab that brain-box.
But how does it connect up?
Like so?

BUTT [*making strange noises*]:

You must sing a-down a-down
And you call him a-down-a –

HAROUN:

I've driven it mad.
Let's see . . .

BUTT:

Look, look! A mouse. Peace, peace!
This piece of toasted cheese will do it.

HAROUN:

Third time lucky, I hope.

BUTT:

So what took you so long?
Let's go. Va-va-voom!

HAROUN:

They'll kill us if we try to escape.
We've only got one minute left of the Bite-a-Lite.

IFF:

Look in your right pocket.

HAROUN:

What? Wow! I'd forgotten.
There's still some wishwater left.

IFF:

Go ahead. Wish us out of this mess
If you think you can concentrate.

HAROUN:

Maybe this time I can do better than that.

IFF and BUTT:

Remember
The harder you wish
The better it will work.
Your heart's desire
Will be as good as yours.

HAROUN:

I wish – what will I wish?
My wishes fly before me
Like a school of flying fish.

I wish this moon to turn
I wish this moon to turn in such a way

Today
Right now
So that the sun will shine
Shine on the Dark Ship
Shine on the dark Chupwalas one by one
Shine on, Oh sun
Shine on the bad
Shine on the good
Shine on the world, the work of Khattam-Shud
Shine on the poisoned sea
Shine on my friends and shine on me.

I wish – this is what I wish.
My wishes fly before me
Like a school of flying fish.

I wish the sun to rise
Shine on the dread Chupwalas with their negative
   eyes
Shine on the Dark Ship on the poisoned sea
Shine on my mother wherever she may be
Shine on my friends, shine on my dad, and shine on
   me.

   [The sun rises and the Dark Ship is destroyed.]

Scene Five
Meanwhile, at the Citadel of Chup

CHORUS:
War! War! War! War!
War between the lands of Chup and Gup!
War between the lands of Gup and Chup!
A battle to the death!
A battle to the dying breath!
A struggle for the triumph of the forces of the good!
A struggle for the overthrow of
Khattam-shud!

> *[Battle music, culminating in final deflation of the Chupwalas.]*

PRINCE BOLO:
Where are you, Khattam-shud?
Come on out.
Your army has been defeated
On the plains of Bat-Mat-Karo
And Batcheat
My golden girl
My princess, my love –
Where are you? Are you still alive?

DEFEATED CHUPWALA:
Listen a moment.
You'll soon hear where your girlfriend Batcheat
    waits.

BATCHEAT:

Oooh I'm talking 'bout my Bolo
And I ain't got time for nothin' else.

RASHID:

I'm sure I know that song
But the words seem different.

BATCHEAT:

Lemme tell you 'bout a boy I know,
He's my Bolo and I love him so.

BOLO:

She sings? My Batcheat sings?
Then hush my friends and hearken to her song.

BATCHEAT *[appearing at a window in a tower]*:

He won't play polo,
He won't fly solo,
Oo-wee but I love him true.
Our love will gro-lo,
I'll never let him go-lo –
Got those waiting for those Bolo blues.

BOLO:

Beautiful. That's so beautiful.

BATCHEAT:

His name ain't Rollo,
His voice ain't low-lo,
Uh-HUH!
        But I love him fine,
So stop the show-lo,
Pay me what you owe-lo.
I'm gonna make that Bolo

Mine
YESSIR!
I'm gonna make that Bolo – aaggh, mmfff –

> *[Khattam-shud appears at the window, his*
> *hand over Batcheat's mouth.]*

KHATTAM-SHUD:
Prince Bolo, General Kitab,
I have heard your idle boasts
And it is true that my army has suffered a trifling
    reverse
But before I let anyone lay hands on me
I shall sew up the lips of Princess Batcheat
And put a stop to this racket for good
By sacrificing her to the colossus of Bezaban.
I have the needle here!
I have the thread.

PRINCE BOLO:
Someone help me. Help save the Princess Batcheat!

CHORUS *[looking at their fingernails]*:
Well . . .

BATCHEAT *[breaking free for a moment]*:
I'm gonna MAKE THAT BMFFF!!!

BOLO:
Is that a voice or what is it?

RASHID:
It must be a what-is-it
For it isn't a voice.

> *[Rumbling noise in distance.]*

KHATTAM-SHUD:
  Maybe this staple-gun will do the trick!

CHORUS:
  That sounds like an earthquake!

  [Sun rises on Citadel of Chup. Enter Haroun
  with Iff, flying on Butt.]

HAROUN:
  It's a Princess Rescue Story.
  It's a deed of derring do.
  It's a case of death or glory –
      A priori
  It's my cue.

CHORUS:
  It's a well-known category.
  It's a tale that's tried and true.
  It's a Princess Rescue Story.
      A priori
  It's our cue.

  [They rescue Princess before Citadel collapses,
  taking Cultmaster and Idol with it.]

Scene Six
At the Door of P2 C2 E House

HAROUN:
  They told me to report here
  And they sounded cross

Maybe I'm in trouble.
Knock knock.

VOICE:
Who's there?

HAROUN:
Haroun.

VOICE:
Haroun who?

HAROUN:
Haroun who was told to report here.

VOICE:
Come in, little Haroun.
Come in and get a big surprise.

HAROUN:
Is it a nice surprise
Or a nasty one?

VOICE:
It's a *surprise* surprise.
It's a

　　　[The door opens. Light floods the stage.]

CHORUS:
Party! It's a party!

Hats off to you, Haroun.
Hats off to you, Haroun.
You're a heck of a chap
In a heck of a spot.
Hats off to you, Haroun, Haroun,

Haroun!
Haroun!
Hats off to you, Haroun.

RASHID:
When you've lost your inspiration
And you've story-teller's block
And you're somewhere between a hard place
And the proverbial rock
When you need a chap to befriend you
Or you'll burst like a stuck balloon
I can heartily recommend you
My talented son, Haroun, Haroun –
You're a tonic!
You're bionic!
My talented son, Haroun.

CHORUS:
Hats off to you, Haroun, etc.

PRINCESS BATCHEAT:
When they drag you off and gag you
And bind your every joint

CHORUS:
Stop!

BATCHEAT:
In a Princess Rescue Story
Which seems to have lost its point,
When you suffer a dread enforcement
And you feel you're about to swoon
I can offer a warm endorsement
Of my punctual friend Haroun, Haroun –

I was frantic!
You're romantic!
My punctual friend Haroun.

CHORUS:
Hats off to you, Haroun, etc.

IFF, BUTT, BOLO, etc:
For that deucedly difficult mission
For that quasi-impossible quest
For his verve and vim and vision
For his zip and zeal and zest
From the top-knot to the toenail
From pigtail to pantaloon
We can offer a testimonial
For our capable friend Haroun, Haroun –
Your example
Has been ample,
Our capable friend Haroun.

CHORUS:
Hats off to you, Haroun, etc.

THE KING:
Haroun Khalifa,
To honour you for the service
You have done to the peoples of Kahani
And to the Ocean of the Streams of Story
We grant you the right to ask of us
Whatever favour you desire
And we promise to grant it if we can.

RASHID:
Well, Haroun, any ideas?

HAROUN:

It's no use asking for anything
For what I really want
Nobody here can give me.

THE KING:

I think we can give you what you want.

HAROUN:

And what would that be?

THE KING:

After a great adventure
Everyone wants a happy ending.

HAROUN:

A happy ending, yes.
But not only for me.

I come from a sad city
From the sad city of Alifbay.
I should like a happy ending
Not just for my adventure
But for the whole sad city too.

THE KING:

Haroun, Haroun
Happy endings come
But not till the end of the story.
I think – ahem –
That you and your father here
Have forgotten something.

HAROUN:

What could that be?

RASHID:
>   Oh my goodness!
>   Snooty Buttoo!
>   It had quite gone out of my mind.
>   Come, Haroun, there is no time to lose.

Scene Seven
Mr Buttoo's Rally

CHEERLEADERS:
>   Vote Buttoo
>   Vote Buttoo
>   Who's the one for you?

>   Not just one, Buttoo!

MR BUTTOO:
>   All the people will vote for me
>   Whether they like or no –
>   The muddy peasant with his ruddy wife,
>   The butcher with his bloody knife,
>   The nice boy on the way to school,
>   The ice-boy with his ice-chopping tool,
>   The master of the silver band,
>   The lowly crematorium hand –
>   All the people will vote for me
>   Several times in a day.
>   None of them will get away
>   Until they vote for me!

CHEERLEADERS:
Vote vote vote
For you know who.
Vote Buttoo.
Vote Buttoo.
Vote Buttoo, or else!

BUTTOO [*aside to Rashid*]:
And you, Mr Rashid,
You're on now,
And you'd better be good, or else . . .

TWO MEN IN MOUSTACHIOS:
Or else out comes that tongue from your lying
throat.

BUTTOO and TWO MEN:
What a pity
What a horrible pity
What a horrible pity that would be.

RASHID:
Ladies and gentlemen
The great Shah of Blah
The Ocean of Notions himself –
That is, myself –
Is about to tell you a story
And the name of the story I am going to tell is
Haroun and the Sea of Stories.

CHORUS:
Tell us that story!
Tell us that story!

HAROUN *[aside]*:
 So you didn't forget . . .
 You're back on line.

RASHID:
 There was once a young boy
 In the sad city of Alifbay
 Where the smoke of the sadness poured away
 Poured away
 From all the sadness factories . . .
　　[Continues telling story in dumbshow.]

BUTTOO:
 I don't like the sound of this.
 I don't like the sense of this.
 I don't like the mood of this.
 I don't like the tense of this.

CHORUS *[listening to Rashid]*:
 No-o-o-o.

BUTTOO:
 I don't like the drift of this –
 Something slipping away from me.
 I don't like the shift of this –
 Someone calling it a day for me.

CHORUS:
 Ah-a-a-ah! No-o-o!

BUTTOO:
 I want the glory and
 I want it whole,
 I want a storyline
 I can control.

Control
Control
I can control!
I want a storyline
I can control!

MEMBER OF CHORUS:
Mister Buttoo
Khattam-shud!

CHORUS:
Yes.
Mister Buttoo
Khattam-shud.

BUTTOO:
All right everyone –
That's enough story-telling.
Now everyone go down to the polling-station
And vote for me!
Vote for me!

CHORUS:
No no no.
We will not vote for you.
We will not speak by rote for you.
We will not trail a coat for you
Or push out the boat for you
Any more.

BUTTOO:
How can this be?

CHORUS:
    Because we are free –
    Or we shall be soon
    Thanks to the efforts of Haroun.
    We shall be free of you for good.
    Snooty Buttoo is Khattam-shud.

    [They chase him away.]

Scene Eight
Back Home

RASHID:
    Here we are, son,
    Back home again in Alifbay.
    I wonder what we'll find.
    Hallo? Anyone there?

HAROUN:
    Miss Oneeta, Miss Oneeta.

MRS SENGUPTA:
    Oh, too fine.
    You are back. You are back.
    What celebrations we will have,
    What sweets there will be to eat!

HAROUN:
    Why, what is there to celebrate?

MRS SENGUPTA:
    Well now, for me
    I have really said goodbye to Mr Sengupta.
    I'm finally and truly empowered
    And I am free as a bee.
    And as for you . . .
    You know . . .
    Someone else has said goodbye to Mr Sengupta too.

RASHID:
    Soraya! My dear wife!

SORAYA:
    I know, I made a mistake.
    I went – I don't deny.
    I acted like a fool
    Or worse
    And with that snivelling drivelling
    Mingy stingy
    Measly weaselly clerk.
    But now he's done for
    Done for good.

HAROUN:
    Khattam-shud.

SORAYA:
    That is right, Haroun, my son.
    Mr Sengupta is Khattam-Shud.

RASHID:
Welcome home, Soraya.
Welcome.
Welcome home.

Scene Nine
Haroun Wakes in his Bedroom at Dawn

SORAYA'S VOICE:
Zembla, Zenda, Xanadu
All our dreamworlds may come true –
May come true
They may come true
All our dreamworlds may come true.

HAROUN:
Where am I? Who was that?
Oh
That was my mother singing.
I must be home after all.
I was afraid it was all a dream.
    [Picks up toy Hoopoe.]
And my friend, my friend the Hoopoe,
So small now he can fit in my hand.
Please understand
My friend
It's good to know
You will be here if I should need you.
You'll be ready to go.
But I've had enough adventures for a while.

HOOPOE'S VOICE:
  But but but . . .
  No problem.

SORAYA'S VOICE:
  Fairy lands are fearsome too
  Fearsome too
  Fearsome too
  Fairy lands are fearsome too.

  [All the clocks in the house begin to strike six.]

HAROUN:
  What's all this?
  I have a new clock
  New clothes and presents.
  Of course, it must be my birthday.
  Time is on the move again.

SORAYA'S and RASHID'S VOICES:
  As I wander far from view
  Read and bring me home to you
  Home
  Home
  Bring me, bring me home to you,
  Again.

HAROUN:
  Everything rhymes.
  Everything chimes.
  Yes, time is on the move again!

THE FALL OF JERUSALEM

An Oratorio by Dominic Muldowney

I

NARRATOR:
It was a time of peace. Prosperity
Hung in the air
As bright as dust in the sun,
When Jesus, the son of Ananias, came to the Temple
For the Feast of the Tabernacles.
He was an ignorant nobody, a very ordinary fool.
Suddenly he began to shout.

JESUS:
A voice from the East
A voice from the West
A voice from the four winds
A voice against Jerusalem and the Sanctuary.

A voice from the East
A voice from the West
A voice against the bridegroom and the bride.
A voice against all the people.

NARRATOR:
Day and night Jesus wandered the alleyways
Shouting these words of ill omen
Until the citizens became angry
And they beat him repeatedly
But he said nothing in his own defence
Only

JESUS:

A voice from the East
A voice from the West
A voice from the four winds
A voice against Jerusalem and the sanctuary

A voice from the East
A voice from the West
A voice against the bridegroom and the bride
A voice against all the people
Alas for Jerusalem

NARRATOR:

And they led Jesus to the magistrate
And they whipped him till he was flayed to the bone
But he never begged for mercy
And only continued his cries
So they took him to the Governor Albinus
Who said:

ALBINUS:

This Jesus is nothing more than a common maniac.
Release him at once.
He's done no harm to anyone.

NARRATOR:

And so for seven years and five months
Jesus continued his cries.
He never cursed the men who beat him
Nor blessed those who offered him food.
But, when the Romans laid siege to Jerusalem
And Jesus saw his prophecies fulfilled,
He found his peace at last

And for the last time
He uttered his cry:

JESUS:
Alas again for Jerusalem
Alas for the people
Alas for the Temple
And alas, alas for me also.

NARRATOR:
At this, a rock from a catapult
Struck Jesus and killed him at once.

II

CHORUS:
The God of quake and thunder
Who holds you in his beak
Will tear you from the sheepfold
And carry you to the peak
And show you where the legions
Are massing on the plain
And bid you warn the people
Of pride and plight and pain.

The God of blight and famine
Who holds you in his claw
Will make of you a prophet
And smite you on the jaw.
And you shall speak in silver
But they shall turn away

And you shall sing in sapphire
But they shall hear in clay.

The God of death and duty
Who crushes you with his arm
Will scald you with his beauty
And make his love your harm.
What sin of yours inspired him
Thus to descend to prove
The danger that has fired him
The scandal of his love?

III

NARRATOR:
Now when the Emperor Nero heard the news
Of the defeat of Cestius
And the disasters in Judaea
He was secretly alarmed
And he sent Vespasian to command the armies in
    Syria.

So God was shaping the destiny of the Empire.

And Josephus was governor in Galilee
When Vespasian arrived
With all his legions and eagles and ensigns,
His archers and slingers,
His horsemen and his battering-rams.
And Josephus knew in his heart
That the only safety for the Jews

Lay in submission
And he pleaded with the Jews.

JOSEPHUS:
All that my dreadful dreams foretold
All that I feared has come to pass.
The God that made our people great
  Will cut us down like grass.

Broad is the empire, strong the foe,
Hard is the hand and fierce the pride.
You say that we must fight. You know
  That this is suicide.

God sees we scorn the gift of life
And he will hate us on that score.
The God who made our people great
  Will punish us the more –

Punish us in the life to come,
Punish the children yet unborn,
Punish us for this suicide,
  Punish us for this scorn.

NARRATOR:
But they answered:

CHORUS:
God it was who gave us our minds,
Minds that scorn death,
Scorn to live in slavery
Under a Roman yoke
Josephus, is life so dear to you
To face a life of slavery,
A life of dishonour.

Well may the laws of our fathers groan aloud
And God himself hide his face for grief.

NARRATOR:
And Josephus said to himself

JOSEPHUS:
These are men who want to die
But I,
I shall live,
I'll escape to the Romans.

IV

CHORUS:
We saw the flaming chariots in the sky.
We heard the Romans and their battle-cry,
The crack of the whip, the rattle of the wheel,
The bright sword flashing with the burnished shield.

The ring of fire, the burning walls
The silver running down the doors,
And all that treasure, all that gold is gone –
Gone like the gold of Solomon,
Gone like the gold of Babylon.

Their horses are swifter than leopards.
And fleeter than the evening wolves.
They shall fly as the eagle that hasteneth to eat.

Ladder, spear and crowbar come,
Turtle shield and battering ram –
Tell me what a fool I am

And what a sinner I am,
Hated of God,
Hated of God,
Hated of the Lord.

The wolf is in the sanctuary
The leopard is at the door
The eagle is at the carrion.
 We are carrion.
 We are carrion.
The Sanctuary is no more.
 It is reviled.
 It is defiled.
The Sanctuary is no more.

V

CHORUS:
 Jerusalem, Jerusalem
 Where is that great city now?
 Where are the ramparts?
 Where are the towers?
 Where is the city founded by God himself?

 Jerusalem, Jerusalem –
 She is torn up by the roots
 And her destroyers have pitched their camp in her
  ashes.
 The old men weep among the ashes of the Shrine
 And the women wait for the last humiliation.

VI

MEN:
>Never to see the sun.
>Never to feel the flame.
>Never to see the sun
>>Shine on our shame.

>Never a child shall live
>Slave to a Roman lord.
>Never a woman shall grieve.
>>We have a sword.

>We that alone survive,
>We that are hated of God,
>We have our sacred laws.
>>We have a sword.

>Father and wife and child,
>Mother and child and shame,
>Father and blade and sun –
>>Father and flame.

>We shall be tall as fire
>Deep as our destiny –
>We that are hated of God –
>>We shall be free.

VII

CHILDREN:
>Jerusalem, Jerusalem
>The prophecy came true.
>Oh tell another story
>Of the life we never knew.

>Oh tell us another story
>And tell us you were wrong –
>We never saw Masada
>Nor the Roman throng.

>We never saw Masada.
>We never heard the name.
>For we stayed out till sunset
>Playing a skipping game.

>And we stayed out till sunset
>And we were in a dream.
>We never heard our mothers
>Calling across the stream.

>Jerusalem, Jerusalem,
>Now we can hear you call –
>Calling us as our mothers did
>While the shadows fall.

Acknowledgements

The Love Bomb was originally commissioned by the Royal Opera House, Covent Garden.

The commissioning of *Haroun and the Sea of Stories* was made possible with support from the Ann and Gordon Getty Foundation, the Evelyn Sharp Foundation, the Heinz Foundation, Laurence Lovett, the Mary Flagler Cary Charitable Trust, the National Endowment for the Arts, the Peter Jay Sharp Foundation and Louisa Sarofim.

The Fall of Jerusalem was commissioned for the millennium by Leeds Festival Chorus and Southampton Philharmonic Society. Funds for Leeds Festival Chorus were provided by the John S. Cohen Foundation, the R. M. Burton Charitable Trust and Yorkshire and Humberside Arts. Funds for the Southampton Philharmonic Society were provided by the Britten-Pears Foundation. The music is by Dominic Muldowney. The first performance was given by Leeds Festival Chorus, Leeds Festival Chorus' Youth Choir and the Leeds Schools' Choir with the BBC Philharmonic, conducted by Simon Wright, at Leeds Town Hall on 11 March 2000. The second performance was given by Southampton Philharmonic Society, Southampton University Choral Society, Highcliffe

Junior Choir and King Edward VI School Choir with the New London Sinfonia, conducted by David Gibson, at Southampton Guildhall on 31 March 2000.

Among the people who have helped finding collaborators for *The Love Bomb* I should like especially to thank Howard Stokar in New York, and John Caird, Jane Glover and Roger Graef in London.